The Spirit of
Rawtenstall

Waterfoot, Newchurch and the Whitewell Valley

Kathy Fishwick

Kathy Fishwick.

Published by

Landmark Publishing Ltd
Ashbourne Hall, Cokayne Ave, Ashbourne, Derbyshire DE6 1EJ England
Tel: (01335) 347349 Fax: (01335) 347303
e-mail: landmark@clara.net
web site: www.landmarkpublishing.co.uk

ISBN 1 84306 069 8

© **Kathy Fishwick 2003**

The rights of the author to this work has
been asserted by her in accordance with the Copyright,
Design and Patents Act, 1993.

British Library Cataloguing in Publication Data: a catalogue
record for this book is available from the British Library.

Print: Bath Press, Bath
Design: Mark Titterton
Cover: James Allsopp

Front cover: Rawtenstall centre from Hall Carr, October 1979. Rothwell's Longholme Shed is in the foreground, right, now the site of 'Focus' D.I.Y. Store. St Mary's School is immediately to the left of the chimney. (Arthur Percival)

Title page: Aerial view of Rawtenstall Centre in 1963. The small centre island is the hub of traffic control, with the bus station to its right on the site of the old 'Grand', later 'Palace' theatre. The newly-built supermarket replacement for Longholme Sunday School (now 'Boots') stands out clearly on the left as do the extensive roofs of Longholme weaving shed right of centre. The railway track on the right has now been replaced by 'Bocholt Way', the by-pass named after Rossendale's German 'Twin Town'. (D.H.)

Back cover top: A group of Scouts drums the Home Defence Corps through the Square. (J.D.)

Middle: This outing was to promote the Players' production of "Ring Round the Moon" in 1959, and was taken just off Bacup Road in Rawtenstall, with Cawl Terrace Co-op in the background. (R.C.T.)

Bottom: By the 1840s, the population of the Whitewell Valley was enough to merit a new church; it was built in 1848 by the architect James Clarke in the Romanesque rather than the then popular Gothic style, in a dramatic setting atop a prominent hill. (J.D.)

LANDMARK COLLECTOR'S LIBRARY

THE SPIRIT OF
RAWTENSTALL
Waterfoot, Newchurch & the Whitewell Valley

THE 20TH CENTURY IN PHOTOGRAPHS

Kathy Fishwick

Landmark Publishing

Contents

Foreword by Janet Anderson MP

This book is essential reading for everyone who knows and loves the Rossendale Valley, and for visitors who seek to learn about our history. What a wealth of information is contained here. Rawtenstall, Waterfoot, Newchurch, Whitewell — names which may mean little to Valley outsiders, I urge readers to dig deep into these pages because they will help you to understand the world that is the Valley of Rossendale and the history that has made our people what they are today.

Rossendale is a proud and independent community. When I first came to the Valley in 1985 Rossendale produced one-third of the UK's output in slippers and shoes. The Rossendale Union of Boot, Shoe and Slipper Operatives was the last remaining of the small trade unions which represented our manufacturing industries. Those strongholds, remnants of the industrial revolution which made our valley a force to be reckoned with have long since gone. But the spirit of the people remains.

Rossendale Valley folk are the warmest, the kindest, the most down to earth and pragmatic I have ever had the privilege to know. They take the knocks, bounce back, get on with life — and always make sure they live life to the full.

This book details essential parts of our history in the 20th century. The visit of King George and Queen Mary to Rawtenstall. Trickett's Memorial Ground in Waterfoot, funded by voluntary contributions from the slipper workers in memory of those who lost their lives in the First World War. Dame Clara Butt's performance at the Palace Theatre; the children from Salford who sought refuge in Rossendale during the Second World War; the Walking Days in the 1950's; when Rossendale United played Bolton Wanderers in the FA Cup in 1971; the demolition of Longholme Mill — now the Asda supermarket; the Rossendale Male Voice Choir who won at Llangollen four years in succession; Jimmy Heyworth and his band whose memorable performances at the Astoria Ballroom are still a topic of conversation among those who remember.

This is the Rossendale Valley we know and love. To understand our Valley folk, you have to know their history. Kathy Fishwick's contribution to that and her work for the Civic Society deserve to be recognised. This pictorial history is a testament to Kathy's knowledge of and love for our Valley. It is record of which we are immensely proud.

Janet Anderson MP

Acknowledgements

Footnotes

Rawtenstall was a Borough in its own right including Cloughfold, Waterfoot, Newchurch and the Whitewell Valley, itself a collection of small individual settlements, until merger with Bacup and Haslingden to form Rossendale Borough Council in 1974. References in this book to "the town" mean the old Borough of Rawtenstall, to "Rossendale" or "the Valley" means the new Borough or the geographical area.

The north west part of the area, Constable Lee, Crawshawbooth Goodshaw and Loveclough, although also part of the old Rawtenstall and present Rossendale, is not included due to the great amount of material aviable, which would have resulted in fewer pictures of it and the others already involved. It is a deliberate omission in order that more justice can be done to it in a later publication.

Dedication

This book is dedicated to to the memory of John Davies who loved Rossendale and did so much to research and record the history of its hills and mills. Many of the pictures used have been kindly lent by his friend Stephen Spencer. This one shows John in his element, amidst the industrial archaeology of the moors. Thankyou, John.

Pictures not attributed individually are with thanks to

J.D.	John Davis
D.H.	David Hamer
R.Lib.	Rawtenstall Library
R.Mus.	Rossendale Museum
R.F.P.	Rossendale Free Press
R.C.T.	Rossendale Civic Trust (Formerly Rawtenstall Civic Society)
D.W.S.	David Whitehead and Sons Ltd.
K.F.	Kathy Fishwick
R.G.	Ryan Goodwin
J.W.	Joan Whiteley
F.T.	Freda Tomlinson

*All pictures with an asterisk are known to have been taken by the individual named, otherwise they are from that person or organisation's collection.

Introduction

Rawtenstall is my home town. I played in and explored its streets and meadows as a child, and was brought up on the memories and tales of my parents, also life-long citizens. Yet there is always something new to learn and discover, especially from other peoples' perceptions of the area, and what they felt was worth recording.

I knew the late John Davies when he was researching the origins of our mills and pubs, and we often exchanged information, as well as regrets at missing historical records. John donated some of his collection to Rawtenstall Civic Society (now Rossendale Civic Trust), and many of these pictures appear in this book, but it is a collection of John's slides, kindly lent by his friend Stephen Spencer, which really encapsulates images of the old Rawtenstall and Newchurch which I, and I am sure many other people thought had been lost forever. Also busy with a camera during the major changes of the 1960s was Trust member David Hamer, who has contributed a large number of photographs from his personal collection to build up the picture of the town we once knew. It was when it was pointed out to me that pictures I was using for my W.E.A. Local history classes were themselves records in their own right that the idea of a publication came together, and "Landmark's" interest came just at the right time.

In selecting pictures from the many around, in addition to those from private collections, I have tried to choose those that have never, or rarely, been published before. The ones that I have included are because they are either the only one, or the best available on that particular subject. It has been my privilege to act as editor – the pictures speak for themselves.

My sincere thanks go to everyone who has contributed in any way to compiling this book. Acknowledgements are given on every picture, to individuals lending one or a few by name, and by initial to those lending more. This way I hope that no-one has been missed. Others who have helped behind the scenes are Trish Barnfield at Rawtenstall Library, Sandra Cruise at Rossendale Museum, Stephen Spencer, Chris Aspin, Ron Simpson, Mike Clark (who scanned many of the pictures), David Pilling for printing long unseen negatives, Adrian Purslow at Rossendale Free Press, Ryan Goodwin with constant encouragement, Thomas Fishwick as "computer tutor", Janet Anderson for her time in looking through the pictures before publication and writing the "Forward", and the publishers for their patience and the freedom in letting me get on with the job.

Altogether there has been so much interest and co-operation from so many individuals and organisations that the book does indeed live up to its title, and prove that there is a real "Spirit of Rawtenstall" alive and well in the town today.

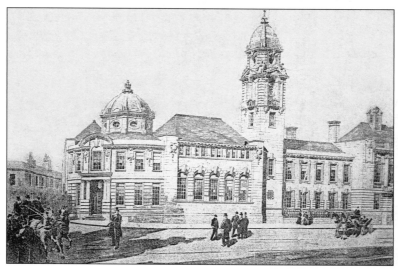

One of the first missions of Rawtenstall Corporation, founded in 1891, was the provision of Municipal Buildings. This was the plan for Queen's Square, with the Library adjoining a prestigeous Town Hall, prepared by architects Crouch, Savage and Butler of Birmingham with Art Nouveau details typical of the period. (R.C.T.)

The Library under construction, probably in 1905. The space to the left was the site of the former St. Mary's Church Vicarage. (R. Mus.)

The Library was the only part of the scheme to materialise, being funded by the philanthoropist Andrew Carnegie. In 1907 he attended the opening ceremony in person, and is seen here in the centre of the group with top hat and white beard. (R. Lib.)

This view was taken in 1961, when it was still possible to cross Haslingden Road without much trouble. The building on the left at this time was the Co-op Furniture Store, one of many Co-op premises around Queen's Square. (J.D.*)

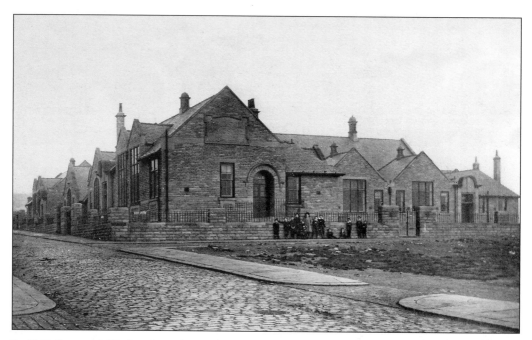

In 1909 Rawtenstall's first Secondary School was opened, taking the name 'Alder Grange' from the nearby "mill owner's mansion" formerly belonging to Joseph Wood Whitehead of Higher Mill. The school had rooms for specialist subjects such as woodwork and cookery, and also took adult students for evening classes. (D.H.)

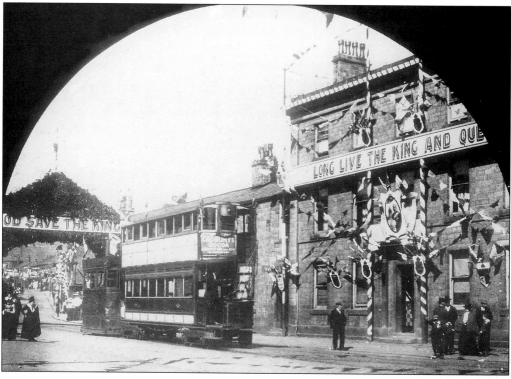

In 1902 the town was richly decorated for the Coronation of Edward VII. Here a steam tram poses outside the Queen's Arms and an arch frames a view of Bank Street to the left. (R.C.T.)

In 1913, Rawtenstall received its one and only recorded Royal visit, from King George V and Queen Mary. A platform was built where the present bus station now stands, and their Majesties arrived in a fleet of motor cars, enough to bring the crowds out in their own right. Note the contrasting backgrounds of Ilex Mill and the open hillside of Hall Carr. (R.C.T.)

All ambitions to develop the town any further were put on hold during the Great War. The railed -off gardens have taken the town hall site next to the Library, and a group of Scouts drums the Home Defence Corps through the Square. (J.D.)

Hundreds of local men volunteered to join the services, especially after the disasterous summer of 1916. A group assembles here on the junction of Bank Street and Lord Street, probably in preparation for the march to sign up in Bury. (R.Lib.)

Rawtenstall Training Corps struggled along for months with very limited equipment and resources before being officially recognised. This picture was taken at their training camp on Dearden Moor for the Rossendale Free Press of September 30th 1916. (R.Lib.)

Edgeside Hall, former home of the Barcroft family, was donated by them to the war effort and used to house Belgian Refugees. Amongst them were skilled decorators who painted the Art Nouveau panels in the offices of Sir H.W. Trickett's slipper factory at Gaghills, Waterfoot. (R.Lib.)

Above: The Great War was a great leveller. Two men from the village of Newchurch won medals for bravery, Pte, A.J.A. Titmas (above left) worked at Trickett's slipper factory and was awarded the Military Medal: Lieut. Geoffrey Bolton, son of the coal-mining magnate H.H. Bolton of Heightside House gained the Military Cross. The village was equally proud of both of them. (R.Lib)

Left: Tom Watson, seen here with his young wife Lizzie, was one of many to leave for the Front within days of getting married. Tom survived the War, although badly shell-shocked, and lived in Richard Street until his death in the early 1950s. Tom had been one of the last pupils at the old Newchurch Grammar School (see p.130) being one of the privileged few to win a scholarship. (K.F.)

Right: On September 25th 1916 a Zepplin appeared over Rossendale seeking its way to Manchester. It dropped several bombs in the area, one near a farm at Lumb and another near Lea Bank, but caused no deaths or injuries. This incendiary bomb failed to ignite, and is preserved in Whitaker Park Museum, displayed here by curator Sandra Cruise. (R.F.P.)

Above: War Memorials became a feature of towns, villages and churchyards; this one was unveiled in 1921 in front of Longholme Sunday School, now the forecourt of Boots Chemists. The wall at the top right can still be recognised as that of the cake shop. (R.Mus.)

Left: Rawtenstall is now recognised as having the first War Memorial in the country to be erected by the community, being inspired by Alderman Carrie Whitehead in 1915. Erected in the Cemetery, its status is now recognised by the Imperial War Museum and as a Listed Building after research by local historian Bill Turner, here laying a wreath. (Bill Turner)

In Waterfoot, the workpeople of Sir H. W. Trickett's donated part of their wages to purchase a section of the former Thistlemount Estate for a Memorial Garden. (See p.119) It was opened on September 30th 1922. (R.C.T.)

Under pressure in WW1, Rossendale proved it could cope; although a traditionally poor agricultural area, this field of wheat was grown at Sagar Holme, Lumb, as part of the War effort. (R.C.T.)

Rawtenstall did not have an official War Memorial until 1929, when Carrie Whitehead was Rawtenstall's first woman Mayor. It is a simple obelisk of Shap granite, in the Library Gardens ('Sparrow Park') with a bas-relief panal by L.B. Roslyn of London, in the style which became typical of many other fine monuments of its kind. (R.C.T.)

This Memorial is quite rare in as much as it includes women and children. Guarded on each corner by a member of the Armed Services, it acknowledges nurses, farm and munitions workers, as well as those left to carry on after the loss of husbands and fathers. (K.F.*)

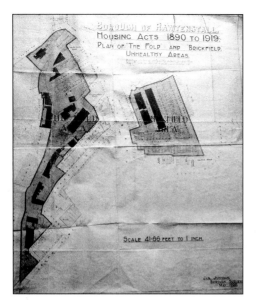

Left: After the War, municipal works were again put in hand, especially the clearance of slum dwellings under the various Housing Acts. The main areas to be targeted were the old Fold and Brickfields, to the East and West of the now main thoroughfare of Bank Street. Residents were re-homed in the first Council houses to be built, at Higher Cloughfold and Hall Carr. (R.C.T.)

Below: The Fold had grown up along the old winding road by the River Limey, so narrow as to need replacing by Bank Street as early as the 1820s. This picture, although taken in 1950, still gives some indication of its character, overshadowed by the mill buildings of David Whitehead and Sons. On the left was the school opened by the Whiteheads in 1838, later the Astoria Ballroom, and on the right was Martin's Bank, which formed the junction of the Fold with Bank Street. (R. Lib.)

The housing conditions in the old Fold can be appreciated here; hastily thrown up to house factory workers before the health concerns of the 1840s. This is the junction of the Fold with Back Lane, the building in the centre being later replaced by the 'Wheatsheaf'. This is now the line of the by-pass which swept through in the 1960s. (R.C.T)

The lane that connected the Fold with Tup Bridge was known as Market Street, and here the houses stood with their backs on the edge of the river. This is roughly where Whiteheads built their new weaving shed in the 1920s, which was latterly the pine furniture salerooms. Not all these children would be close family; children would often be looked after by distant relatives and neighbours. (R. Lib.)

The 'Wheatsheaf' stood on the corner of Back Lane and Market Street, one of a batch of inns in the the older top half of the town. The Harrison family were licencees for many years. Back Lane, now almost lost in the middle of the car park, was the main link with Hurst Lane and the farms of Chapel Hill long before the Turnpike Roads came through in the 18th anf 19th centuries. (J.D.*)

The other old inn in the Fold was the 'Sun' , on the corner of Lord Street West. Unlike the Wheatsheaf, this was never altered, but like the Wheatsheaf it survived until the 1960s, retaining the proportions of the old town into living memory. Despite its unpretentious appearance, the 'Sun' was the chosen survivor of the two, its successor being built on Bank Street after demolition for the by-pass. The 'Wheatsheaf ' has never been replaced. (R. Mus.)

The time between the wars was one of 'getting back to normal', and here the Lancashire Fire Brigade Friendly Society holds its 48th "Annual Demonstration" on June 2nd, 1923. Mr. Herbert Sanderson's "Dirty Dozen" won First Prize of £2.00 in the "Humourous; Jazz and other Bands" section. The procession went from the Roe Buck at Lumb to Queen's Square, Rawtenstall, and here they are on their way back along Bacup Road, near today's Health Centre and semi detached houses. Alder Grange School is silhouetted on the skyline to the right. (R. Lib.)

Rossendale has always been known for its musical excellence, and choirs and concert parties abounded, often based on the churches, chapels and Sunday Schools. This is the organist and choir of Kay Street Baptist Church in 1926. (R.C.T.)

Local people also loved a good play, and regular performances were given at the Unitarian Church at Newchurch. This is the cast of one of the "New Year" plays of the 1920s. (R.G.)

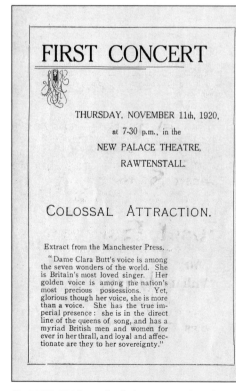

FIRST CONCERT

THURSDAY, NOVEMBER 11th, 1920,

at 7-30 p.m., in the

NEW PALACE THEATRE,

RAWTENSTALL.

COLOSSAL ATTRACTION.

Extract from the Manchester Press.

"Dame Clara Butt's voice is among the seven wonders of the world. She is Britain's most loved singer. Her golden voice is among the nation's most precious possessions. Yet, glorious though her voice, she is more than a voice. She has the true imperial presence : she is in the direct line of the queens of song, and has a myriad British men and women for ever in her thrall, and loyal and affectionate are they to her sovereignty."

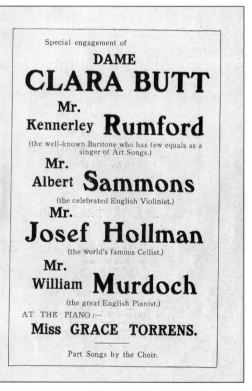

Special engagement of

DAME

CLARA BUTT

Mr.
Kennerley **Rumford**

(the well-known Baritone who has few equals as a singer of Art Songs.)

Mr.
Albert **Sammons**

(the celebrated English Violinist.)

Mr.
Josef Hollman

(the world's famous Cellist.)

Mr.
William **Murdoch**

(the great English Pianist.)

AT THE PIANO :—

Miss GRACE TORRENS.

Part Songs by the Choir.

Sir H.W. Tricketts had their own choral Society, but attracted national celebrities to their Concert Programmes. In November 1920, they secured the services of Dame Clara Butt, whose voice was descibed in the programme as "one of the seven wonders of the world." Accordingly, the New Palace Theatre in Rawtenstall was booked for the performance, prices raging from £3. 0s. 0d. for a box to 2s. 4d in the unreserved area. All proceeds went to the Memorial Gardens at Waterfoot. (See earlier.) (R.C.T.)

Above: The 'Palace', originally the 'Grand' Theatre, had a fairly short and unremarkable life. It dominated Queen's Square until 1937, and originally had a market hall attached, just visible here as a gable end to the left of the bus. This gave its name to Cheapside, a street which survived it by 30 years. (R.Lib)

Left: The theatre was said to be cold and draughty, with poor sightlines, and by the 1930s was being used by the local companies rather than visiting acts and celebrities. When it was finally demolished, no-one seems to have mourned its loss. Its site was taken for the bus station, with a view to creating a transport interchange with the nearby railway station. (R.Lib.)

The time between the wars was also a time for people to take advantage of new opportunities. Rawtenstall's trams had been replaced by buses which not only provided links with the surrounding Lancashire towns, but went further afield as well. The Annual Outing must have been the original "busman's holiday" when they were joined by their families for a special excursion, Blackpool, Morecambe or Southport being favourite destinations. The assembly point for this gathering in June 1937 is still easily recognisable as today's bus station. (K.F.)

Church and Chapel were still a major part of life. The gathering here is the Bible Class and Middle Sunday School in St. Mary's school hall in the late 1930s. This magnificent building had a large gallery with classrooms underneath, separated by wood and glass partitions that could be folded back to give flexible space. It was used regularly for major civic functions as well as for the day and Sunday Schools, and many an old scholar remembers the badminton court, having been told to "stand on the white line" for the attention of the headmaster after misbehaving. (Terry Horrocks.)

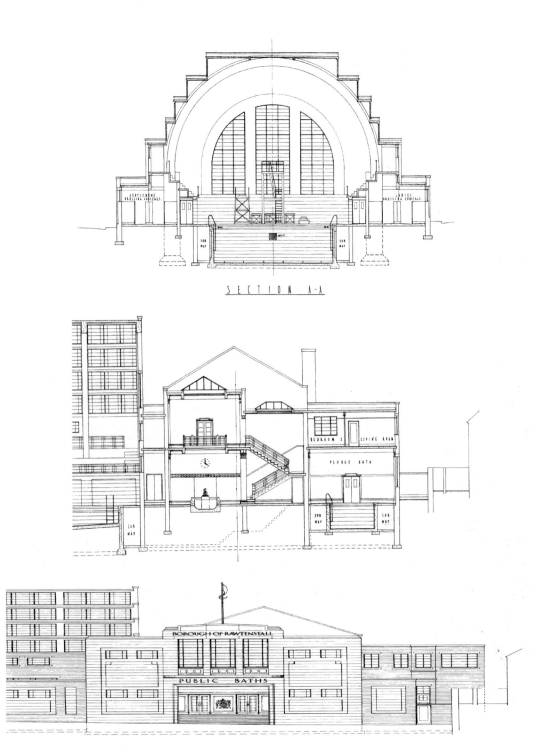

SECTION A-A

GENTLEMENS DRESSING CUBICALS.   LADIES DRESSING CUBICALS.

SUB WAY   SUB WAY

BEDROOM 2   LIVING ROOM

PLUNGE BATH

SUB WAY   SUB WAY

SUB WAY

BOROUGH OF RAWTENSTALL

PUBLIC BATHS

Ambitious plans continued to be drawn up. Of the three valley towns, Rawtenstall alone had no swimming bath, and one was planned to put the others to shame. On the cleared site of Brickfields, this massive Art Deco structure would have been totally out of scale with the surrounding houses of Daisy Hill and South Street, but the designers ignore this in their self-indulgence. The large pool is lit by stepped tiers of windows, there is a small "plunge", cafe, flat for caretaker and family, and a decorative fish pond in the foyer. The site remained undeveloped, and is now a car park. (R.C.T)

Once more, wartime restrictions held up development – no transport interchange, no baths. This time War was coming closer to home and drastic measures were necessary for air raid precautions. *Above:* Shelters were dug in the Library Gardens as a town centre refuge, but many people put their faith in the underground quarries, these below being prepared at Scout. (R.Lib.)

Refugees from Salford arrive at Rawtenstall Railway station. As with the WWI Zepplin, German aircraft often circled over Rossendale, "playing" on route to Manchester or Liverpool, but no serious or deliberate bombing raids hit Rawtenstall. (R.Lib.)

Left: In the 21st century, the revived Rawtenstall Railway hosts re-created War time events. Amongst the participants on one occasion was this evocative little chap as a refugee complete with gas mask and attache case with personal treasures tucked in amongst his required change of underwear. (R.G./R.Lib)

Right: James Robert Fuller stands proudly in his uniform outside Lower Hawthorne Head Farm (often known as "Doldrums" due to its sheltered position on the slopes of Cribden). Robert was killed in action in 1944, aged 21. He had been in the forces for three years. (K.F.)

Rawtenstall's adopted ship was HMS Fancy, an Algeric Minesweeper, 'flat' type, built in 1943. She displaced 950 tons and carried 100 crew, was one of the leading ships on 'D' Day and by 1944 had swept 233 mines. Ex- Petty Officer George Wilkinson wrote in 1987 – "No one except those who served at sea will know how grateful we were for the gloves, scarves, helmets and games we received from the good people of Rawtenstall." (R.Lib.)

In February 1945 'Fancy' returned the favour by adopting St. Mary's C. of E. School. The crew sent skipping ropes and toys made on board, and the canteen fund provided the 1945 Christmas Party, seen here in progress in the school hall (R.Lib)

Above: By 1946 the Sunday School processions and carnivals had begun again. All denominations had their walks, and sometimes, as here, combined for real impact. Accompanied by Brass Bands and Scout drums, they always brought out the crowds. (K.F.)

Left: Longholme Methodists parade down the top part of Bank Street, the children under the banner of "God's Jewels". The Co-op Hall is behind the banner on the left, and the chimney of "Star" Mill behind. The original cobbled surface of the street has been exposed again recently after many years under tarmac. (R.F.P/. K.F.)

The firm of David Whitehead and Sons not only successfully survived the war, but was about to become one of the nation's leading fabric producers. Their employees worked hard and played hard, especially when departments rivalled each other at carnival procession time. These floats from June 8th 1950 show their skills and the lasting wartime influence. (R.C.T./ DWS)

St. Mary's Sunday School Scholars line up in the old school yard for Walking Day in 1951. Mothers toiled for hours over the white dresses with blue sashes and the canvas shoes were carefully whitened at the very last minute to ensure perfection. The pink, white and blue flower arrangements were pleasures and treasures in their own right. (K.F.)

The Festival of Britain in 1951 gave the whole year a carnival atmosphere. Rawtenstall's grand procession began on Townsend Street at Waterfoot, progressing down the valley to the cricket ground at New Hall Hey. St Mary's Sunday School class was presented as "God's Garden", seen here by the path to Ivy Cottages. The blond haired boy in the centre foreground is Stuart Holt, later headmaster of Clitheroe Royal Grammar School. (K.F.)

Rawtenstall centre on a perfect early summer day in 1957. Even Whitehead's chimney has stopped smoking. The gardens, now with railings and rhodedendrons removed and replaced with well-laid out flowerbeds, were the envy of many other local towns. (J.D.*)

Looking towards Queen's Square and the Queen's Arms Hotel, 1957. Although officially known as the "Library Gardens", the more friendly local name was "Sparrow Park". (J.D.*)

The parks department excelled at commemorative displays, which could be seen to full advantage on the sloping bank. (J.D.*)

In 1966 there were three displays, the main one commemorating 75 years as a Borough. It was also the last time that the displays would be possible; the following year saw the start of the great upheaval. (J.D.*)

The 1950s were Rawtenstall's hey-day. The Astoria Ballroom attracted dancers from all over East Lancashire. The frontage on the street became Rawtenstall's first fashionable Coffee Bar, complete with frothy cappucinos. To the left, Burnley Building Society occupies the former gate house to Holly Mount, home of the Whitehead family and later the offices to Lower Mill; to the right, Martin's Bank stands on the junction of Bank Street and the Fold. (See page 18) (Clarence Hoyle/ R. Mus.)

The 1930s band in their Art Deco setting - Bert (?) on tenor sax, Styx Isherwood on drums, Freddie Durst piano, Eric Arnot on trumpet and Jack Cannon on double bass. Eric Arnot was wages clerk and time-keeper at Howard and Halstead's bakers. (Bob Waddington)

Jimmy Heyworth's band was generally reckoned to be the best in the country in the late 1950s, although visitors included Joe Loss, Edmundo Ross and Eric Delaney, as well as stars such as Dickie Valentine and Lita Rosa. It was also the venue for several local functions and legendary children's Christmas Parties. Visitors to the Astoria came from all over East Lancashire and Rawtenstall Corporation Motors put on special late-night buses to get people home to Burnley, Accrington and throughout the Rossendale Valley. Right up until its closure in the mid 1960s, this was the place to be. The replacement Astoria over the new shopping precinct, never captured anything like the atmosphere of the original. (Lancashire Evening Telegraph/K.F.)

Astoria advertisement from the Rawtenstall Borough Handbook of 1957. (K.F.)

BOROUGH OF RAWTENSTALL

Elizabeth R
1953

Coronation
SOUVENIR
PROGRAMME

Price Sixpence

SATURDAY, 30th MAY (continued).

10-15 p.m. THE ARENA, WHITAKER PARK.
(if wet, in St. Mary's School, Rawtenstall)

Musical Pageant

Elizabeth I to Elizabeth II
in
Tableaux, Music and Dance

Presented and Arranged by the
Rawtenstall Borough Arts Association

Honorary Producers :
John J. Haworth, John Stansfield, Harold Foulds, John Shires,
Jack Davey.

The Company :
Members of Local Amateur Organisations with the assistance of
the British Legion, St. John Ambulance, Girl Guides, Boy Scouts,
Public Services and Civil Defence.

Musical Continuity by Goodshaw Band
(Conducted by Mr. E. Kershaw)
and
The Rossendale Male Voice Choir
(Conducted by Mr. F. Tomlinson).

The Script written by Mr. H. I. Hunt, Borough Librarian.

Lighting, Wardrobe, Make-up and Stage Assistants by Members
of the Association.

PAGE TWENTY-SEVEN

1953 brought the Coronation, and another spate of carnivals and processions. The programme cover was designed by Jack Catlow, the then Borough Treasurer, whose skills in calligraphy were called on for presentation certificates for many years. (K.F.)

Programme above, cast below. The highlight of the week was the Pageant in the Park, with an open air performance involving leading local choirs, actors and brass bands. (R.C.T)

For the Coronation Procession, the workers from Whiteheads again turned their hands to creating spectacular floats. *Above:* A celebration of the nations of Great Britain and the commonwealth into which Whitehead's trade was rapidly expanding. *Below:* Whiteheads celebrated their own break-through into the market of contemporary furnishings, presenting the ultra-modern living room to people coming out of the post-war gloom and restrictions of rationing. (D.W.S./R.C.T.)

Rawtenstall had two cinemas, the Pavilion, dating from 1911 (but on the site of an earlier one) and the Picture House, a superb example of provincial Art Deco by a local architect named Brocklehurst. It was later converted to provide Bingo and Snooker facilities, as well as being used as a location venue for the film "Girls' Night", but at the time of writing is converted to shops which remain empty. (J.D.*)

PICTURE HOUSE

Tel. 123—Under the Management of J. J. Theatres, Ltd.—Tel. 123.

To-day (Saturday) at 2-30, 6-0 & 8-30—

CINEMASCOPE
ROBERT MITCHUM, MARILYN MONROE in

RIVER OF NO RETURN

(Cert. "U")   In Technicolor.

ALSO FULL SUPPORTING PROGRAMME

WEEK COMMENCING MONDAY, MARCH 28th, 1955

Monday 2-30 & 7-30. Tuesday & Wednesday 7-30—

Children under sixteen not admitted.
VALERIE HOBSON
GERARD PHILIPE   JOAN GREENWOOD in

THE KNAVE OF HEARTS

(Cert. "X")

ALSO FULL SUPPORTING PROGRAMME

Thursday & Friday 7-30. Saturday 2-30, 6-0 & 8-30—

ESTHER WILLIAMS
VAN JOHNSON   TONY MARTIN in

EASY TO LOVE

(Cert. "U")   Colour by Technicolor.

ALSO FULL SUPPORTING PROGRAMME

PAVILION

Tel. 36—Under the Management of J. J. Theatres, Ltd.—Tel. 36.

To-day (Saturday) at 2-30, 6-0 & 8-30—

GEORGE MONTGOMERY, TAB HUNTER in

GUN BELT

(Cert. "A")
Colour by Technicolor.

ALSO FULL SUPPORTING PROGRAMME

WEEK COMMENCING MONDAY, MARCH 28th, 1955

Monday 7-30. Tuesday 2-30 & 7-30. Wednesday 7-30—

JOAN LESLIE
VERA RALSTON   FORREST TUCKER
JOHN RUSSELL   PAT O'BRIEN in

JUBILEE TRAIL

(Cert. "A")   Colour by Trucolor.

ALSO FULL SUPPORTING PROGRAMME

Thursday & Friday 7-30. Saturday 2-30, 6-0 & 8-30—

RICHARD GREENE   PAULA RAYMOND in

RETURN of the CORSICAN BROTHERS

(Cert. "A")

ALSO FULL SUPPORTING PROGRAMME

Adverts from the Rossendale Free Press in March 1955. The Picture House usually had the best films, for which it was neccesary to book seats in advance, and the Pavilion was home mostly to 'B' movies and cowboy films. (R.F.P.)

In 1956 the local youth were treated to "Rock Around the Clock" – at the Pavilion, where it was thought that they could do least damage. Although this bunch of "Teddy Boys" looks quite excited, no serious incidents occurred. (J.D.)

In 1962 musical aspirations were still traditional, and the brass group from Bacup and Rawtenstall Grammar school played early morning fanfares on May Day from the towers of Newchurch and, here, St. Mary's. Rawtenstall, led by music teacher Michael Nuttall. The selection included "men of Harlech" and "Old Hundredth", the group here being Gordon Hinton, Garth Bradshaw, Jennifer Holt, David Clegg, Richard Holt, Terry Brandon and John Iveson. (K.F.).

St. Mary's day school class - 3A - of 1952. Pictured with the group is Headmaster Mr. Ashburner, who retired that year. In the back row of girls, fifth from Mr. Ashburner, is Heather Taylor (Skillings) who was herself to become deputy head of the school in the 1980s. (K.F.)

St. Mary's equivalent year group from 2002, in a new school and wearing uniform.
(St. Mary's C. of E. School.)

Longholme Sunday School produced regular plays and pantomimes throughout the 1950s, 60s and 70s. These two are from 1953 and 1955. (Barbara Horrocks.)

Safe Cycling for all was a major aim, and annual proficiency tests were held to ensure good road skills. Alder Grange schoolyard was the start for the Saturday morning runs, this one dating from the early 1950s. (D.H.)

Borough Librarian Jon Elliott presents prizes at Lord Street Methodist Sunday School Centenary in 1958. (S. and L. Longworth)

Rawtenstall Council in 1958. Alderman A.H. Howarth is Mayor, with Deputy William (Bill) Nuttall to his left and Town Clerk Graham Thomas to his right. (S. and L. Langworth)

Rossendale began 'Town Twinning' in 1952 between Bacup and Bocholt, but the first time Rawtenstall joined in was in 1963. Here on April 18th, the German visitors meet Council Officials, including the Mayor, Bill Nuttall. (S. and L. Longworth)

The most outstanding success of the 1950s belongs to Rossendale Male Voice Choir. Under their conductor Fred Tomlinson, they won the international Eisteddfod at Llangollen three years in succession – 1952, 1953, and 1954. Here, Fred is chaired by his singers as the result is announced at Llangollen in 1954. (F.T.)

The Cricket Field was an ideal place to rehearse for open air performances. The choir is here on a very serious dress rehearsal complete with bow ties and wing collars. Fred later wrote to the Rossendale Free Press to thank all the employers who allowed the men time off work to take part. (F.T.)

At a concert at St. Mary's School on December 8th 1953, Fred Tomlinson was presented with an illuminated album by the Mayor, Alderman Harry Turner, as an appreciation of the honour brought to the town. The Town Clerk is Jack Blomeley. (D.W.S./R.C.T.)

The presentation was followed by an hour long concert, attended by the Mayors of other local Boroughs and Rossendale's M.P. Tony Greenwood, seen here sitting next to Fred's wife May (in the chequered dress). He described the choir as "the best ambassadors that Rossendale had ever had." (F.T.)

Tony Greenwood, later Lord Greenwood of Rossendale, was one of the Valley's most popular figures. He was both the mill-girls' pin-up and a most efficient Member of Parliament. Here he shares a joke with his Conservative opponent, John Parkinson, in the Mayor's Parlour at Rawtenstall Town Hall just before the 1955 election. Tony was returned with a majority of 2,911. (R.C.T.)

New Hall Hey Cricket Field has long been a regular venue for carnival events as well as cricket matches. This picture, taken in 1962, shows the then nearly new College building dominating the scene in its original five storey block format. (J.D.*)

Labour Party Gala, 1963. A large procession of Morris dancers, Majorettes and costumed characters turns off Bury Road onto New Hall Hey Road. The building in the background (left) is the former railway goods shed, now J.A. Taylor's Car Show Rooms, and Rawtenstall East Signal box is just behind the brass band. (J.D.*)

Hardman's Mill at New Hall Hey now stands in a fairly open setting, but until the 1960s it was surrounded by various smaller workshops and worker's houses. This terrace, always with neat little gardens, stood on the site of the car park to the present "Cobblers" restaurant. (J.D.*)

The terrace in the previous picture stood on the sunny side of the lane; here is the opposite side just before demolition. These old woollen workers premises contrast with the then new industrial building in the background, beyond the level crossing at the top of the slope. Rawtenstall West Signal box is on the left. (Ron Hoyle* /R.C.T.)

Hardman's Mill in its original setting, with the lodges that provided water for the various processes. The one in the middle of this picture held clean water for the finishing process and was known as 'Swanny Lodge' from the graceful inhabitants who lived there for many years.

There has been a mill on the site since the 1770s, the present one dating from 1861 after the old premises were burnt down. The architect was Richard Williams, brought by the Hardmans to Rawtenstall after working on the Houses of Parliment in the 1840s. Williams built many prestigeous local buildings including Hardman's own house at Horncliffe, which are now listed. The mill chimney survived a Public Inquiry into possible demolition in 1980 and is now recognised as one of the best in Lancashire. (Clarence Hoyle*/R. Mus)

Left: The large, shallow lodge was used to good effect in the Coronation celebrations. (D.W.S./R.T.C.)

Left: and as if to join in, that same year the swans produced a brood of cygnets. (D.W.S./R.C.T.)

1951

Left: The 1950s were also the best years of David Whitehead and Sons Ltd. at Lower Mill. They became leaders in the post-war fabric design revolution, setting the pace with exhibits in London for the Festival of Britain in 1951. Daring and experimental designs were produced by artists including the young Terence Conran, and "architectural " prints from amongst others, John Piper. These fabrics are now recognised as classics of their time and have an honoured place in 20th century design history – examples being on display in the Victoria and Albert Museum in Kensington. (D.W.S./R.C.T.)

Below: Whiteheads were also pioneers in social care at their factories, especially Lower Mill. Even in the 1940s, they had creche and nursery facilities for employees' children. (D.W.S./R.C.T.)

Gone were the days when factory workers had their lunch brought in by a young or retired family member. Whiteheads had a canteen and dining room, serving well-balanced meals in a civilized setting, which could also be used for plays and presentations. (D.W.S./R.C.T.)

Tell that to the tacklers! "Tacklers", the men who mended and maintained the looms, were a breed apart; their sense of humour and tall stories were notorious. This group at Whiteheads in 1954, gathering in their cabin with milk bottles and straws, may be out to make some comment on a now long-forgotton situation. (D.W.S./R.C.T.)

Above: On the 7th of September, 1955, Alhaji the Sardauna of Sokoto visited Lower Mill to sign an agreement with Whiteheads. He was the Prime Minister of the Northern region of Nigeria, which was seeking to attract new industries, and Whiteheads were chosen to build and manage a mill manufacturing Nigerian cotton. Far from seeing this as a threat to Lancashire's industry, Whiteheads saw themselves competing with the growing sales of Indian cotton, and clawing back some of the African market.

Kaduna Textiles was born, and Whiteheads are still there, long after Lower Mill has closed. The signing took place in the board room at Holly Mount, which was the original home of the Whitehead Brothers and later became the Company's offices. David Whitehead and Sons Ltd still exist and retains some property interests around the town. (D.W.S./R.C.T.)

Left: Due to many reasons, the Lancashire Textile industry had gone into irreversible decline by the mid-1960s. Mrs. Eileen Marsh, the last weaver at Lower Mill, "wove out" at no. 3 Shed in July 1967. It was the end of an era. (R.Lib.)

Left: On Saturday, July 18th 1964 Rawtenstall was hit by serious floods which swamped the town centre and caused thousands of pounds worth of damage. The rivers, unable to cope with the effects of a cloudburst over the moors, burst their banks and water swept down the streets like a tidal wave. The Fold was a natural channel to the bottom of Bank Street, where pedestrians gathered in groups waiting for the water to subside. (R.Mus.)

The Rossendale Free Press reported: "It was a fantastic scene with vehicles of all descriptions marooned in the middle of it. A bus stood at an odd angle across the road and cars were dotted about like boats in a strange, brown lake". (R.Lib)

Left: On Burnley Road, householders dragged their sodden carpets out to dry on the Cemetery Wall. It was many weeks before things returned to normal, but the late 1960s and early 1970s were to bring changes that would alter the face of the town for ever. (J.D.*)

Above: In the late 1960s, the long- smouldering desire for the major development of Rawtenstall became alight again with the plans for the national Motorway network, the M66 envisaged as linking Manchester and Burnley along the Edenfield, Rawtenstall and Crawshawbooth route. This resulted in the complete clearance of the town centre, including New Hall Hey Hall and New Hall Hey House. The Hall dated from the early 1600s and had been neglected since the transport interchange proposals of the 1930s. (R.C.T.) *Below:* The later House had served as a Hospital during WW1, but neither was allowed to stand in the way of progress and demolition took place in June 1967. (R.Mus.)

The remains of the two houses lie by the side of Haslingden Road, much mourned by local people and a source of anger to historians. The Hall itself was one or Rossendale's then few Listed Buildings, and its demise was included in the influential "Loss of the Country House " exhibition at the Victoria and Albert Museum by ' SAVE' Britain's Heritage in 1974. (Ron Hoyle*/ R.C.T.)

A view the opposite way, of the town centre from the then new Accrington and Rossendale College. The 'Pavilion ' and Ilex Mill are on the right - the gable left of centre is the back of Grand Buildings, on Cheapside, soon itself to be bulldozed away for the huge centre island. (D.H.*)

Left: Crossing Queen's Square on foot would never be safe again. The solution was a sub-way under the whole width between Haslingden and Bury Roads, with a branch seen here, leading onto the central island, still at that time envisaged as a potential bus station. This part of the subway, which has always been a problem, was closed off in the early 1990s due to fears of vandalism, but by then it led only to the new fire station. (J.D.*)

Below: The proposed motorway took a huge swathe through the town using the route of the old Fold, clearing the few remaining buildings that survived the 1920s, and also the Astoria and a large part of St. Mary's Churchyard. Over four hundred bodies, mostly dating from the mid 19th century, were exhumed and re-interred in the cemetery. On this picture, the original churchyard wall can just be seen, still standing, with "Church Pad" carried over the excavations by a temporary bridge. (J.D.*)

Above: The bottom row of shops on the western side of Bank Street, with Martin's Bank, was also a victim of the new road. Here in 1962 they are unaware of their fate. All were demolished except the one on the far end on the right. Generally known as the "Fent Shop" it sold sewing goods and haberdashery. It now stands alone as a betting shop, opposite Nat. West Bank, at the remaining corner of Lord Street West. (J.D.*)

Above: The opposite side of the street was demolished for a new precinct, utilising space where older houses had been cleared behind (see later). However, this meant losing some of the original businesses, including Fentons, the nearest thing Rawtenstall ever had to a department store, selling ladies and children's clothes on two floors. (J.D.*)

Below: The entrance to tody's precinct is roughly on the site of Lord Street, seen here with Freeman Hardy Willis on the corner.

The top end of this row of shops is now the site of the replacement Sun Inn. (J.D.*)

Above: Back Bank Street, from Lord Street looking south, an idea of the small, cramped back -to- back houses labelled as slums in the 1957 Housing Act, and prime candidates for the local clearance programme. This is roughly where the present Post Office stands in the precinct. (D.H.*)

Above: Hargreaves St. was right across the middle of today's precinct. Some of the hollows that appear in the car park are where the in-fill of the cellars has settled. (J.D.*)

Right: Back Bank Street from Lord Street looking north. The steps lead up onto Kay Street, not very far from where the steps from the precinct do today. (J.D.*)

Above: The future shopping precinct site completely cleared, with the old Police Station and Courts about to follow. The former Post Office, now sorting office, can be clearly seen on Kay Street (J.D.*)

Rossendale was home to many Non-Conformist groups and the Primitive Methodists (left) and United Methodist (right) both stood on the old Lord Street. Support had dwindled by the 1950s and by the time these pictures were taken in 1963 the united Methodists had become a decorator's store. (J.D.*)

Right: Part of the "hinterland" between the Town Hall and Bank Street, seen from the fire escape at Longholme Chapel. The "Dutch Gables" right of centre are the old Rawtenstall Corporation Tram Sheds; the flat roofed building in the foreground is the then new Hamer's Funeral Parlour. Ilex Mill is in the background. (D.H.*)

Left: The same area, coming down to ground level, from outside Hamer's. This is James Street with Hargreaves Street, Richard Street and Haslam Street going off to the right. (J.D.*)

Right: The Tram Shed cleared with the Primitive Methodist Chapel on Lord Street exposed behind. (J.D.*)

Left: In March 1964 the Corporation hosted the Holcombe Hunt on the site of the old Tram Shed. They went on to hunt over Chapel Hill and Higher Cloughfold, raising a couple of hares but without a kill. (K.F.*)

Right: The Tram Shed site became home to a modern extension for the Town Hall, built by the long-standing local firm of Ashworth and Hobson. Hamer Street still stands, bricked up prior to demolition, behind, with Hamer's on the left. (D.H.*)

Left: The extension, one of Rawtenstall's then rare "modern" buildings, was designed by Council Architect Peter Nuttall, and merited a mention in the North Lancashire edition of Pevsner's "Guide to the Buildings of Britain". Remarkably the gates to the former tram-shed still survive on James Street to this day. (J.D.*)

Longholme (Wesleyan) Methodist Sunday School started in 1816, this later building adjoining the new chapel of 1842. Until 1909, it was also the main day school for Rawtenstall under longstanding headteacher Mr. Dunkin. The cramped conditions were relieved by the building of Alder Grange (p.11). It was an early casualty of the changes, being demolished in February 1962. Note the War Memorial from p.15. This is now Boots, the trees still standing on the forecourt. (J.D.*)

A bulldozer sits on the pile of rubble that was the Sunday School, against the back corner of the chapel. Hamer's joiner's shop and Wesley Villa are the other buildings behind. (D.H.*)

Left: The demolitions continued apace into the 1970s and early 1980s, one late casualty being Rothwell's Longholme Shed, now 'Focus' D.I.Y. This view up the River Irwell, also showing the Pack Horse Bridge, was taken in 1976. (K.F.*)

Below: The Pack Horse Bridge carried the road from Bury into the Town before the turnpike roads of the 1820s met in Queen's Square. When the railway cut across it in 1846, it became almost forgotton. When the railway closed and the site of Longholme Mill became 'Asda', the bridge came back into its own as a pedestrian route to the store. Now carefully paved and restored, it is another of the town's Listed Buildings. (K.F.*)

A typical November day on Bury Road in 1967, just before the clearance of another group houses classed as 'slums'. The block on the right is now the site of the New Hall Social Club and row of shops. The lack of traffic makes it hard to believe that a by-pass could have then been considered necessary. (J.D.*)

An early clearance choice was Mill Street, along with Water Street, at the bottom of Hall Carr Road. This is now the site of "Asda's" loading bay. Note the massive block of "Dicky Deb's" (MASCO) Longholme Mill behind. (J.D.*)

"Dicky Deb's" was Richard Ashworth, "Dick, son of Deborah" in local dialect. The mill dated back to the early 1800s, but in its later days became Mitchell, Ashworth and Stansfield and Co., producing carpet underlay. Trade failed in the early 1970s and the mill demolished after the machinery was removed. The remaining derelict site was part of Rawtenstall's darkest days, but was used here as a publicity shot by "Asda", campaigning for their new supermarket site. (R.F.P./R.Lib.)

The cleared site from Bocholt Way in October 1976, looking across the route of the old road from the Pack Horse Bridge to Bury Road. (K.F.*)

As rebuilding gradually started, things came back into shape; Rawtenstall Civic Society, founded in 1974, drew up plans for "Old Fold Garden" on the site of the Astoria, and arranged for the Whitehead School date stone to be brought back to the site, by the newly revealed school clock tower. Above left, the stone in its original position in 1962 (J.D*) Above right and below, being brought back, May 8th 1979. (K.F.*)

Even whilst the old Astoria and shops on Bank Street were still standing (foreground), the new Shopping Precinct and Astoria replacement were rising on the site of Richard, Haslam and Hargreaves Streets. In the middle distance is the modern brick block of the new Courts and County office building on the site of the former Alder Grange House and Conservative Club. The picture is taken from the top of St. Mary's Church tower. (D.H.*)

An earlier picture, from the late 1950s, of the new Accrington and Rossendale College being built at Captain Fold, across what was known as 'Cow Lane', a popular walk down to New Hall Hey Mill and the riverside. Longholme Mill still stands in the middle distance. (D.H.*)

October 1978, and the cleared town centre is still empty. The motorway did not, after all, come through, and the closure of the railway to passenger trains, together with highway safety concerns finally put paid to the transport interchange. Often said to be the largest traffic island in the country, it became a source of political argument and embarrassment for several years. (K.F.*)

The indecision about the centre and inability to settle on a future for the space brought about much public comment and this protest, captured on film by Clarence Hoyle, was an expression of frustration. It was finally sold to Lancashire County Council for a new Fire Station, which was opened on April 26th 1989. (Clarence Hoyle*/R.Mus.)

The shopping precinct in its early form, completely open to Bank Street, in the late 1970s. The 'Fent Shop', at that time an Indian Restaurant, and Lower Mill can just be seen behind the 'Bisto' advert. (K.F.*)

The flower beds and seats were removed from the precinct in the 1980s, when new shops were created on the Bank Street side, and the surface re-laid. Embedded in the paving were markers for a sun-dial, the "hours" to be "caught" by the statue of a little girl playing hoop-la; a delightful idea, except that she was always in the shade! The developers later sold the precinct and took her with them, hopefully, to a new place in the sun. (K.F.*)

The top end of the town was also decimated by the new road, which took the line of the old Fold, but was destined never to get much past Tup Bridge. This remarkable picture shows the cleared length from Tup Bridge to the bottom of Bank Street, with Ormerod Street and the former Unitarian church supported by heavy piling as the bank (from which Bank Street took its name) was weakened by the earthworks. (Clarence Hoyle*/R.Mus.)

The junction of Ormerod Street with Lord Street West – now the car park area behind National Westminster Bank. The old Sun Inn is just off the picture to the left. (J.D.*)

Ormerod Street was a mid 19th century solution to the problem of housing factory workers. Seemingly an ordinary terraced row from the front, it was more of an apartment block, the houses here being "back-to-back" (sharing a central party wall) with a parallel row which also topped two more storeys beneath. Counting the chimney pots is a clue! (K.F.*)

Although backing into the earth, these were not actually "cellar dwellings" as their facade was completely clear. In later years these premises became stores and workshops for local tradesmen. (K.F.*)

A view from the "back balcony" over Lower Mill. The railings included tall posts at various intervals on which to hang washing lines. These pictures were taken just before demolition in 1978, at the very end of the Council's twenty year clearance programme. (K.F.*)

Hall Street in May 1976; the hall being the Co-op Hall on the left. Some of the buildings here date from the days of the old Fold, but were not demolished until the 1980s. Whitehead's extensive Lower Mill has also continued to be lost in bits and pieces, and this cramped scene is at the time of writing an open car park. (K.F.*)

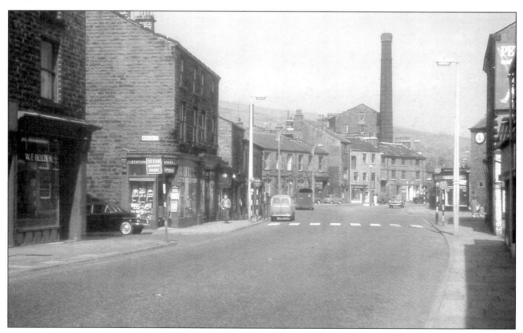

The top of Bank Street, leading to Tup Bridge, in 1962. This is the oldest part of the town, the factory chimney belonging to the former water-powered Corn Mill, later known as the "Star" shoe factory. The building in front of the chimney to the left was a small workshop with a "takin' in" door, and the one to its right the once notorious "Lodgings" or "doss house". (J.D.*)

Tup Bridge is the crossing point of Newchurch and Haslingden Old Roads, joined in the 1800s by Burnley Road. Its name is derived from a sheep market that grew up there in the late 1600s, possibly in context with visits to the nearby Corn Mill. This view in 1962 shows Lamb's greengrocers (with advertising hoarding), a remarkably rickety building well remembered for its piles of loose vegetables and well-worn floor-boards. When demolished, its beams were said to be "soft as cheese". On the left is Dickinson's Chemists, whose own brand "Cough Bottle" was a popular local cure-all. This is now a bridal wear studio. (J.D.*)

March 1968 - and Lambs is demolished. Still standing on Newchurch Road is Arthur Cane's furniture store and behind it, the partially demolished Higher Mill. This was the site of Whiteheads' first steam powered mill in 1824, attacked by the rioters in 1826. At the time of its closure it was known as "Grange Mill", producing hair felt. (J.D.*)

The other side of Higher Mill, from Mill Gate, in October 1967. The building on the right was erected on the empty 'Brickfields' site during WW2 and was used for the administration of Ration Books. It later dealt with Social Security matters. This is the site designated for the swimming baths in 1939, now laid out as a car park. (J.D.*)

Just like the centre island at the other end of the town, Tup Bridge was left empty and planless in 1974. The lack of traffic and the absence of traffic lights is now most remarkable, and it was in fact this picture, shown to a local history class, that encouraged the production of this book............(K.F.*)

The White Horse Inn - later Storey's Garage, in 1962. The shop on the far right was the one later occupied by Gorton's newsagents and then Wilcock's Pet Shop. Gortons moved to the corner shop behind the parked van, now selling gifts. The gable end next to the single storey building is now that of the estate agents; at the time of this picture, it was Turner's, who for many years sold high quality linen goods and essential items such as flanellette nighties, "long johns" and "liberty bodices". (J.D.*)

David Hamer (right) and his friend Graham Hodgson dismantle an early petrol pump behind Storey's Garage, amidst the remains of the Fold. David stored the petrol pump for many years before it found a home in a car museum. Behind are the Bishop Blaize Hotel and the old Fire Station on Burnley Road. (D.H.)

Another great, late loss to Bank Street was the first Co-operative Society building in the town. Built after a competition win in 1867 by Maxwell and Tuke (later builders of Blackpool Tower), this structure also had an iron frame, and served as a store, warehouse, meeting and assembly rooms, having a large, open top floor. Here, the town's first demonstration of electric light took place in 1878, lantern slides thrilled gatherings of the 'Blue Ribbon' club, the first silent movies were shown and the Halle Orchestra performed. Later, it became a drill hall for the Home Guard, and after the war, for a short period, a warehouse for the footwear manufacturers' suppliers, Phipps. The ground floor continued as shops, occupied by Whittaker's greengrocers and Holden's butchers, before various later uses, including an amusement arcade, proved unviable and it was abandoned. Compulsorily purchased by Rossendale Borough Council, it was demolished in May 1987, the site remaining as a car park up to the time of writing. (K.F.*)

A pre-bypass excercise in widening and strengthening Tup Bridge took place in May 1951, when the massive girders of the 19th century had to be cut with oxy-acetylene burners. This picture, reminicent of Ford Madox Brown's painting "Work", was taken on Saturday lunch time when the spectators were on their way home for the weekend - the bus driver, in uniform, holding a newly baked loaf of bread just bought from Bridge's is Jack Watson (see p.110). (R.F.P./R.Lib.)

The junction of Haslingden Old Road and Burnley Road in 1962, with Jack Bridge's Cafe and cake shop on the corner. This was previously owned by Twisses, and all products, including bread, were made on the premises. The cafe was a regular dinner time venue for workers from the local factories, and Jack Bridge was a popular performer at Newchurch Sunday School pantomimes, where he took the part of the "dame". (J.D.*)

Left: The "'Ram's Head" and the "Bishop Blaize" were the main hostelries of the old woollen town, Bishop Blaize being the patron saint of wool combers. The "Ram's Head" is now a Listed building, and traditional market town inn, but the "Bishop", rebuilt about 1910, has recently been re-named "Madison Park Wine Bar," catering for a younger clientel. The space opposite the "Ram" is often used for charity collections and political campaigning, with occasionally visiting Morris Dancers and other performers entertaining shoppers on their way to the market. (K.F.*)

Below: Bank Street has a tradition of long-standing traders and loyal customers. The Dawson family had three generations of ironmongers and locksmiths occupying a number of different premises. David Dawson, here with his sister Millie, took over from his father and supplied both handymen and local factories. David was a stalwart of many local organisations, in his younger days a keen rambler and climber, and later the first Chairman of Rawtenstall Civic Society. Millie, as Treasurer of the Society, and her husband Wilf Baldwin, oversaw the restoration of the Weavers' Cottage Heritage Centre in 1978. (R. C.T.)

Left: The surroundings of Rawtenstall have always been pastoral (see coat of Arms p.178) and there have always been good butchers selling home-killed meat. George Horrocks started in Bank Street in 1922, when there were no health restrictions on displaying legs of lamb in the window.

Below: His son, another George, followed in his footsteps, updating the premises with a large window and 'art deco' signage by local sign-writer Billy Elmer. An extension to the shop was later opened up where the wall is to the right, but this is now the frontage to 'Bookworm'.

left: The ultra-clean red and white image of the 1970s was created by George's sons Roger (left) and Terry, who still retained the striking lettering and tradition of home-cooked meats until 2000, a family presence of 78 years in the same shop. In keeping with Conservation Area status they did later re-instate the more traditional front, and the shop is now an interior decorators studio. (All pictures from Terry Horrocks)

Above: Tom Rowe was the last clogger in Rawtenstall, pictured here in "Lancashire Life" in 1969. When his shop closed in the 1980s, most of the contents were brought to the Weavers' Cottage Heritage Centre, where they can still be seen (K.F.*)

Left: Stanley Gorton took the news-agents and stationer's shop over from his father Tom, who had started business in the little hut known as the "log cabin", perched over the river next to the White Horse. As business grew, Tom moved next door, and later to the former furniture shop on the corner of Bank Street and Barlow Street, (see page 75) where he sold his own brand-name products and children's books. (Lancashire Life)

Malachi Fitzpatrick (Lancashire Life) was for many years the proprietor of the "Herbal Health" shop, keeping alive its traditional remedies and above all its specially brewed drinks, leaving it now perfectly preserved as the "Last Temperance Bar" in Britain. Its subsequent owners have all respected its unique character, and as well as a world-wide reputation, it has a strong local clientel who swear by medicinal properties of "Black Beer and Raisin, " "Blood tonic", "Cream Soda" and "Dandelion and Burdock". (K.F.*)

Right: Very much a presence in the Street is "Sunday Best", the clothes shop owned and managed by Jan Shutt, again with national reknown. Jan, who was "Fashion Retailer of the Year" in 2000, selling designer labels to suit all tastes and age, is seen here (left) with Betty Jackson, another Rossendalian, at the London Summer Collection in 1996. (Jan Shutt)

Left: Even before the town centre became a Conservation Area in 1990, Jan carried out major refurbishment to "Jubilee Buildings", sparking off a revival of Bank Street's trade and character. Jubilee Buildings were built in 1887 by the then landlord of the "Ram's Head" Hotel. (Jan Shutt)

Right: In October 1994, Tony Winder and his staff celebrated "Antony and Patricia's" twentyfive years as hairdressers in Bank Street. Tony (right), has also been a local Councillor and Chairman of the Chamber of Trade, but is best known as the instigator and organiser of the Rossendale Motor Bike Show, which attracts over 25,000 visitors to the town in September each year. (Tony Winder.)

Wilcock's "Pet's Corner" also started off in the "log cabin" and, exactly like Gortons, moved into the next door shop by the "White Horse" as business grew, before taking over much larger premises in the Street. They later branched out into gardening supplies and sports equipment. Mrs. Wilcock (kneeling) is seen here serving customers on a sunny afternoon in 1979. George Wilcock was for many years president of Rawtenstall Chamber of Trade. (K.F.*)

One of the longest-lasting businesses in Rawtenstall was Ben Barnes and Sons Ltd., who began in 1905. Their Garage at the corner of Haslingden Road and Schofield Road was the starting point for many a local holiday, and a major service station for cars from the 1920s onwards. (R.Lib)

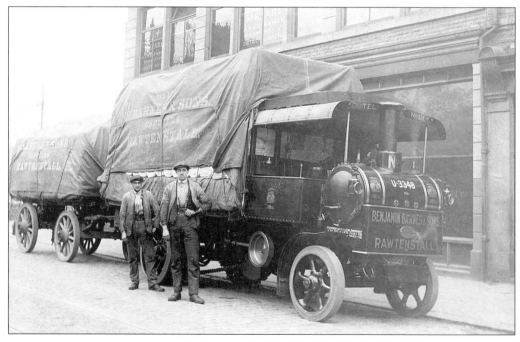

Barnes' started with horses and carts and old Ben was dubious about new-fangled modern propulsion, even the few steam wagons the company acquired in the 1920s, but they certainly trusted them with considerable loads, including trailers with iron-shod wheels. (David Barnes)

Above: The later petrol-driven vehicles served a dual purpose. They could be converted from goods to passenger carrying with interchangable backs. Coach trips were popular in the 1920s and the word "excursion" was no exaggeration, some runs out to the Yorkshire Dales and beyond making full use of the long summer days (David Barnes)

Left: Most people's recollection of Barnes are the sleek cream and green "charabancs" of the 1950s, but Barnes' also ran taxis, wedding and funeral cars. This particular vehicle was a Burlingham bodied A.E.C. with the engine under the floor part way down the chassis. (David Barnes)

Right: For most of its life, Barnes' had contact with the textile trade, and later became part of Coates Viyella, who operated from the Lower Mill site after Whitehead's closure. In its later years, the firm concentrated solely on the haulage business, a smart fleet of wagons in distinctive green and orange livery carrying goods across the nation. The business closed in 2000, when the Lower Mill site was sold. (David Barnes)

Rawtenstall Market was put on an official footing by the new Corporation in 1894, and a Market Hall built soon afterwards with shop frontages to Newchurch Road. It was completely destroyed by a severe fire in 1946, as can be seen from the remains of this shop front (R. Lib.)

An inside market was soon re-established in the war-time storage depot which had been erected on open land behind, and the site of the old market became the present outdoor one. At first, the stalls were temporary, erected and taken down every market day, leaving the space free for parades and gatherings, but by the mid 1950s they had taken on the more permanant form that remains today. Little has changed since this scene was recorded in 1980, except the loss of the chimney on the "Star" mill during its conversion to offices. (K.F.*)

Joe and Edna Gill ran a cooked meat and dairy produce stall on the inside market for many years, famous for its farmhouse "crumbly" Lancashire cheese. Although long under different ownership, the stall is still there. The Jewellery stall was run by Sheila Crowther, who took over from her mother, Mrs Maskell. It was a reliable source of teenage finery and last-minute birthday presents, and again survives under new ownership. (K.F.*)

The market often holds special events when stall holders join in the fun and games. Making a presentation in 1998 is Mayor Molly Disley with her Mayoress Mary Lynch, accompanied by Borough Health Superintendant Sidney Cockcroft (left) and health inspector Dave Walsh, who later worked for a short time himself as market manager. (J.W.)

Rawtenstall was a "Farmer's Market" long before their present popularity. Produce used to be mainly from around Lancashire, especially the market gardens of the Fylde. There are several fruit and vegetable stalls patronised by discriminating locals who can always "tell a good apple by it's skin." This picture was taken in 1979. (K.F.*)

This 1990s Christmas Fancy Dress Competition, brought out the best (and worst!) of the traders' sense of humour. Some have never been seen by their customers as the same again........ (J.W.)

Joan Whiteley (right) has long been the traders' representative on various bodies. Joan's haberdashery stall brings customers from miles around for sewing and craft materials. Her husband Ray took over the biscuit stall, and just to make it even more of a family affair, her daughter Hazel Bates now runs the haberdashery. (J.W.)

In 1997, Dinah Hunt celebrated 40 years on the market, selling books, cards and stationary. Dinah took the stall over from her mother-in-law who started it in 1943. (Dinah Hunt)

Oak Hill Park and the former home of the mill-owning Hardman family was bought for the Borough of Rawtenstall by Richard Whitaker, after whom it has been named ever since. Whitaker Park was opened in 1901, dedicated "to the children of Rawtenstall for ever," and the museum was ready for the public by September 1902. The simple yet classic building seen here about 1910, dates back to 1840, and still retains many of its original features, including some early wallpaper. (R.C.T.)

In the early days, the park was tremendously popular, especially when there was a brass band playing. This view, before the trees matured, shows the single line of houses along Bury Road and open fields behind where Hall Carr estate and Redwood Drive now stand. (Bob Waddington.)

Tea at Spencer's Cafe on Bank Street afer the opening of the summer exhibition in the Museum on May 17th 1927. This distinguished gathering included Alderman Samuel Compston, far right, to whom we are indebted for many good local history records and Hargreaves Wilkinson, ninth from the right, Borough Librarian and museum Curator. The Museum and Library continued to be run independently by the Borough of Rawtenstall until Local Government reform in 1974. (R.Lib.)

Thirty nine years later, in 1966, the Mayor, Councillor Florence Proctor, opens the schools' Art Exhibition, which had become, and still is, a popular annual event. With her are (from the left) Councillor Jim Holt, Chairman of the Library and Museums Committee, Mrs. P. Darbyshire, Art Teacher at St Ambrose (now All Saints High) Secondary School, Jon Elliott, Librarian and Curator, and Mr. S.F. Brooks, Education Officer. (R. Lib.)

"Pop" in the Park, August, 1965. Playing from 2.15 p.m. to 4.30. p.m. were Mercury Recording artists Mike Sax and the Idols and the Diplomats. The event, entirely free, proved a huge success. (R.Lib.)

Crown green bowls is popular in Rossendale and the green in the park is a sun-trap for spending many a leisurely hour, playing or watching. (K.F.*)

In March 1991 Rawtenstall Civic Society, with help from the Royal Mail Anniversary Fund, planted seven young trees in the park to replace those lost to Dutch Elm disease. The Mayor, Councillor Phillip Dunne, and Jack Bell, delivery office manager of Rawtenstall Post Office, do the honours, watched by Society members. (R.C.T./R.F.P.)

In July 1991 the Fountain on the front lawn was pushed over by vandals. Before the Council could count the cost, the Park staff undertook the repair and replacement themselves, preserving it as a major feature in their summer flower displays. (K.F.*)

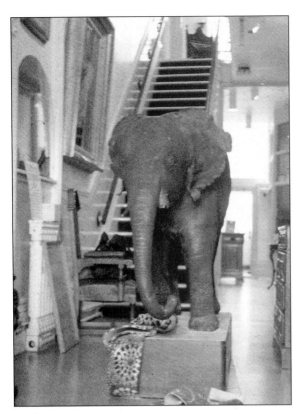

The most popular inhabitant of the museum is Nellie, the baby elephant, whose hide, by the summer of 1989, had been polished by the sticky hands of thousands of local children, her trunk deeply cracked and her tail held on with insulation tape. Fronted by the Friends of the Museum, money was raised for a "face-lift," and she is seen here leaving for the treatment by North West Art Gallery and Museums Services. Nellie is only one of several very old exhibits. When the Museum was opened the collection came from what even the Victorians were discarding, but what are now national treasures in their own right. The contents of Rossendale Museum are a study of museum history itself. (K.F.*)

Whilst she was away, Nellie's place was taken by a carefully crafted replica made by the children of St. Ambrose (All Saints) school. Nellie is the museum's mascot and, although now protected by a glass case, makes her presence felt as a symbol in continuing fund raising campaigns. (K.F.*)

One of the glories of the museum is the mill-owner's re-created lavish drawing room. Children and staff from Water County Primary School re-enacted a visit by factory children to see how their employers lived. (R.Mus.)

In 1991 the Friends held a 90th birthday celebration, with a Victorian Garden Party. In front, in white trousers, is museum caretaker Derek Darlington, with his wife Joyce to his left. They were the last people to actually live in the house, which they left in 1993. (K.F.*)

The rail network reached Rawtenstall in 1846, and ran virtually undisturbed until the 1950s. It was then decided to replace the "Puffing Billies" with diesels, one of the first routes in the country to have such luxury. The date of this picture is believed to be about 1956, with an Independent Television News cameraman filming a train leaving Rawtenstall Station for Bacup. Strangely, the film was never shown in the north. The man in the flat cap on the left is Albert Mathias, long-standing stalwart reporter for the Rossendale Free Press. (R. Lib.)

The level crossing on Bury Road caused many traffic delays and was one of the reasons for the construction of the new road. Ironically, by the time it was completed, the Rawtenstall -Bacup line had been axed by Beeching. On the left is the white gable of the Pavilion Cinema, and on the right the corner of "MASCO", now Asda car park. The rail track bed is now Bocholt Way, and the chimney belongs to Rothwell's Longholme Shed. Picture taken October 8th 1964. (Fred Collinge*)

The level crossing and footbridge at Fall Barn Road, with Ilex Mill in the background. The signal box which controlled the sidings for Ilex Mill and Hall Carr Mills actually stood in the river bed between the rail track and the mill. (Fred Collinge*)

015. Another view of the Fall Barn footbridge and signal box with Albion Mill behind, about 1967. It was the railway that brought Rossendale's industries out of the hills, linking them into a supply line along the narrow valley of the River Irwell. (Fred Collinge*)

Rawtenstall Station looking south in early 1967, after the closure of the line to Bacup. This was the side to wait for the Manchester and Bury trains. The buildings were demolished very soon afterwards, but the platforms, particularly the large edging stones, survived and are part of the platform today. (Fred Collinge*)

The opposite platform, with waiting rooms for Cloughfold, Waterfoot and Bacup in 1966. The new road has yet to come between the railway and the College, which is still seen to its full height behind. (Fred Collinge*)

Demolition of the Bacup platform. Passenger trains continued to run between Rawtenstall, Bury and Manchester until 1977, but by that time they were few and far between and not at all well kept. The coal yard was serviced by goods trains until December 1980, and when they were withdrawn, few people ever thought the line would be used again. (Fred Collinge*)

The same view as the previous picture in 1998. Note the reduced height of the College. A concerted effort by the East Lancs. Railway Preservation Society prevented the track from being taken up and, based on the old Bolton Street Station in Bury, the revival began - and proved that miracles do sometimes happen. (K.F.*)

A date and time was set for the official opening, but the actual honour of being first steam train back, in April 1989 went to the little green engine that had worked so hard for ELRPS over many years. Despite the secrecy that was intended to surround the sneak preview, and the early morning hour, the crowds were out, clambering over the rubble in the old coal yard for a first view. (K.F.*)

The Mayor of Rossendale, Councillor Gaythorne Bland, a former railwayman himself, also presided over the unofficial arrival, making it very much a "locals" occasion. (K.F.*)

The outside of the old station in 1967. The brick structure on the right is the 1950s replacement of the old wooden footbridge. The present station, reconstructed in 1990, is exactly on this site, the cobbled road down the side being retained. (Fred Collinge*)

The same corner in May 2003. The East Lancs Railway runs "Thoms the Tank Engine" weekends which attract the crowds, and the amusement operators. Other events include the very special War-time re-creations, which have included fly-pasts by Spitfires and Hurricanes. (K.F.*)

As an area dependent on wool, the late 1700s saw the growth of three-storey "loomshops" where enterprising employers brought their weavers together under one roof. Few of these buildings now survive in Rossendale, having fallen foul of the "slum clearances" of the 1960s. One that made it through was at Fall Barn Fold, seen here in 1948, surrounded by houses, mill and railway which were all due to disappear within the next twenty five years. (R.C.T.)

Even this building did not survive intact. The back part fell into disuse after 1948 having been the scene of a murder. Maggie Allen, a strange, sad lady, rented the corner dwelling on the right, under the tall, gable chimney. For some reason we will probably never know, she killed an equally enigmatic acquaintance, Mrs. Chadwick, and hid her body in the coal cellar before trying, clumsily, to dispose of it. Maggie was the last woman to be hanged at Strangeways, and the abandoned part of the house was demolished in 1972. (R.C.T.)

Seen here in 1969, still intact, the building, now widely known as the "Weavers' Cottage" was Listed, which gave protection to the important south-facing front with its multiple windowed elevation. Even so, and despite the concerns of many people, it was constantly under threat until bought by Rawtenstall Civic Society in 1975 for conversion to a Heritage Centre. (R.C.T.)

In the 1920s, the building was divided into four seperate dwellings one in each corner. An elderly lady, Mrs Rowe, recalled in the 1970s that she lived here as a child, her bedroom being over the corner by the footpath. She contracted diptheria, and whilst she was lying ill, the pavement outside was covered in straw to deaden the noise of mill-workers clogs as they passed on their way to the facrories in the early morning.

In the 1950s, the front part of the building had been kept in good order by the Millward family, seen here in about 1954. Mr. Millward was the manager of Freeman, Hardy and Willis in Bank Street, but also had an interest in and advised on herbal medicines. Both the young Millwards, whose children and grand-children have since visited the building, as well as the later inhabitants the Duckworth family, said it was always a very happy and pleasant family home. (R.C.T.)

Restoration was far from easy. The building needed to be partly gutted and re-roofed. Inch by patient inch and mainly by volunteer man-hours, it came together again. Society member Edna Winstanley weighs up the size of the problem on the top floor in 1978. (K.F.*)

In August 1990 an authentic spinning wheel was acquired in memory of Chairman David Dawson. Seen here being presented by Mayor Phillip Dunne, and worked by David's sister Millie, it was donated by Clifford Barcroft, himself involved in the spinning industry. Clifford pointed out that it was a strange coincidence that we should be harking back to the origins of our industry in the very week that the last spinning mill in the valley, Smith and Nephew's Glen Mills, was closing down. (R.C.T.)

David Dawson's successor as Chairman, James Sagar, had a wish to see the building full of children learning about their heritage. This group from Sharneyford School, Bacup, acted out a play with music specially written for them by their teachers. The Cottage now plays host to several school visits a year and is open to the public on summer weekends, as well as being a regular meeting place for many groups and Societies. (R.C.T.)

This class from Alder Grange High School not only visited but wrote a report which was printed in the Civic Trust's national magazine. Rossendale Borough Council presented an authentic Victorian steeet lamp, and in 1990 the building was included in the Town Centre Conservation Area. (R.C.T.)

'...and you can take it round
to Carnivals and events...'

In May 2000 the the demolition threat reared its head again, this time for a supermarket car park! By this time the building was too well known to need much fighting for, but local historian and artist John Taylor could not resist putting forward a rescue solution. (R.C.T. / J.B.T.)

Four scale models of the Cottage were made in clay in the early 1990s by local potter Brian Ellis. Only one is now known to exist Here Brian displays one of the models at a local country fair. (R.C.T.)

"My heart leaps up when I behold
The Scented City of Cloughfold"

This panoramic view shows the reason for the schooldays jingle. The Gas Works evolved here in the late 1800s, casting its shadow, and more, over the area until the late 1960s. The Gas ometer and purifying house, left foreground, have now been replaced by housing, and 'Glen Mills' (Victoria Works) to the right by modern factory units. Cloughfold Recreation Ground and Lea Bank are above the gas ometer in the middle distance. (R.Lib.)

Cloughfold had its own station, originally to pick up stone from the quarries, but it later serviced the gas works. Its island platform was not easily accessible to passengers, most of whom were local workers. The railway line was for a long time separated from the road by upright, tarred wooden sleepers, but is now replaced with a landscaped pathway once more allowing a view of the river. (R.C.T)

The new gas ometer erected at Cawl Terrace was for storage, after the works closed in the late 1960s. In December 1968, it is seen here on the right with the old works over the river in the process of being dismantled. (K.F.*)

In the 19th century, smallpox was still a disease to be feared, and Rawtenstall Board of Health erected an isolation hospital off Height End Lane, at Hareholme. As incidents of the disease diminished, the building became superfluous and was demolished by the 1930s. (R.C.T.)

The "Festival of Britain" procession, starting in Waterfoot, gave Cloughfold a rare glimpse of carnival - the float crowned by the gas works is the second prize winner - "A Century of Fashion", entered by Whitehead's Higher Mill. (R.C.T.)

A Christmas story scene seems an odd entry for a summer carnival, but this picture is most interesting for the clothes of the spectators and the old shop fronts behind on Bacup Road - the row called 'Waterside' only recently being able to be seen in that context again with the tidying of the former railway site by the river. (R.C.T.)

Jack Watson in the stores at Smith and Nephew's Victoria Works, 1960. Jack ruled the stores with a rod of iron - not even a box of matches got past him unnoticed. His career included work at several Valley textile mills, and as a driver for Rawtenstall Corporation Motors from 1936 to 1951, when he went to S.and N., staying until retirement at the age of 75 in 1981. (K.F.)

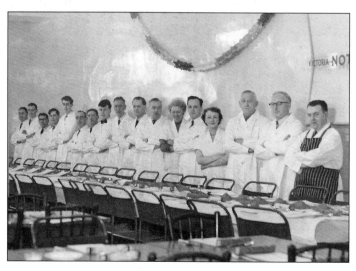

Christmas dinner at Victoria Works was traditionally served to the workers by staff and management. Amongst this 1960s line-up are, third from right, manager Jack Perkins and sixth from right his wife Ada, personnel manager throughout the 1960s and 1970s. (K.F.)

Cloughfold County Primary School is an superb example of Victorian educational provision, retaining many original features. Once hemmed in by other buildings, with little play space, this traditional building now has access to open land behind, and is included in the Higher Cloughfold Conservation Area. (K.F.*)

The Pony Club has met on Cloughfold Recreation Ground for almost 50 years, and is a flourishing organisation. Reputed to have been levelled out by infill of cinders from local mills, the land has now grassed over and affords magnificent views down the Valley to Rawtenstall with its surrounding hills. (K.F.*)

Higher Cloughfold was once the centre of the township of Deadwin Clough, first settled in the 1500s. Old Cloughfold Farm, (left), once the home of the Ministers of Newchurch, was demolished for road widening in the 1920s, but Springhill House remains quietly tucked away on the corner. (R.C.T.)

On the opposite side of the road is the Red Lion Hotel – the old one shown here was replaced in the 1920s. It never closed even for one day, in order to keep its licence, being frequented by farmers and butchers attending the cattle auctions at Johnny Barn Farm. The row of cottages and the Baptist Sunday School immediately behind them still stand, but the Chapel, left, has been replaced by sheltered housing. (Bob Waddington)

Demolished in the early 1980s, the Victorian Sion Baptist Chapel was the successor to earlier meeting places for the local Baptists who trace their origins back to 1675. The sheltered accomodation now on the site is known as Litchford House after the man who first allowed them to use his barn for worship. The Baptists continue to meet in the former Sunday School. (K.F.*)

Ashworth Buildings, seen here from the Chapel graveyard in 1976, were once accommodation for hand-loom weavers, who probably shared the workshop on the top floor. When this picture was taken they were bricked up ready for demolition under the 1960s clearance programme, but saved by Conservation Area designation, and now fully restored to complement the village's status. (K..F.*)

Jottings

James Ormerod, thought to have been a one-time landlord of the "Red Lion", is believed to have committed suicide and therefore could not be buried in sacred ground. His grave, a "table tomb" of 1817, is in a former hen-pen, now allotment, off Dobbin Lane (later re-named Peel Street). It bears the inscription - "When we this good man's life explore, we cannot but avow, what'ere this land had been before, 'tis consrcrated now." "Jottings" was a weekly column in the Rossendale Free Press which covered miscellaneous items including snippets of local history. It was written for many years by Albert Mathias. (R. Mus.)

On the other side of the valley, in the midst of quarry spoil, is a simple carved slab as a memorial to "Lovely", a stray dog who was adopted by the quarry-workers. Dating from 1873 it again bears an inscription in rhyme – "Lovely; On the twelfth of May we laid away one who was loved by many; she hunted rats, was kind to cats, and birds she sought out many." This canine sympathiser sought out the grave on one of Rawtenstall Civic Society's sponsored walks. (R.T.C.)

Cowpe Brook is the only Rossendale river that runs from south to north, cutting through a small valley that has been settled since medieval times. The head of the valley is now dominated by a reservoir, and Kearns Mill, which has its origins in the early 19th century. With Cribden Hill gracing the sky-line, this is one of the quintessential views of Rossendale Valley. (R.T.C.)

For several years in the 1990s Cowpe had its own Country Fair, attracting traditional crafts displays from far and wide. Most of the local residents were involved in the organisation, and this group were entitled to enjoy their well-earned break. (Niel Caygill.)

2003 marks the 100th year on the same site for Kearns. This picture from a 1990s publicity brochure shows the staff of the time with present Managing Director John Ashworth at the end of the group on the right. (Kearns.)

The firm specialises in dyeing yarn, originally woollens, and produces not only perfect colour matches for contract carpeting, but also permanent dyes for cotton and man-made fibres to be woven into checks and stripes where it is important for the colours not to run. Although in old premises, the firm prides itself on up-to date technology. (Kearns.)

On April 28th 1985 a dream came true for Councillor Eleanor Graham, when, as Mayor of Rossendale, she officially opened the Rossendale Way, a circular walk over the hills surrounding the Valley. Eleanor, left, was a tireless campaigner for Rossendale's heritage and environment. With her are former Chief Planning Officer Ian Goldthorpe, seated, and, behind him, Director of Rossendale Groundwork Peter Wilmers. (K.F.*)

Ian Goldthorpe was Rossendale's Chief Planning Officer from 1974 to 1984, but in his own private capacity he researched, wrote and illustrated three books of Rambles around Rossendale's Countryside, highlighting features of special note en route. (R.C.T.)

Hikers celebrate the Rossendale Way opening on the hills above Cowpe, despite a typical blustery and showery April day.

Although noted for their grandeur and scenery, the weather on these moors can be treacherous, and this group are well dressed for the conditions. (K.F.*)

This marker was erected on Top o' t' Leach in 1974 to commemorate the merging of the three Boroughs of Bacup, Rawtenstall and Haslingden into the new Rossendale. Amongst the Rawtenstall Civic Society Sponsored Walk group are (from the right) Irene Sykes, Paul Davies (John Davies' son), local historian John Taylor, Eddie Roberts, Kathy Fishwick and Sheila Pike. (R.C.T.)

Bill and Rachel Kenyon were keen walkers with an extensive knowledge of local buildings and footpaths. They both took part in local events until well into their seventies. (K.F.*)

Another Sponsored Walk, this time over the hills above the Whitewell Valley, on April 1st 1983. The little white dog belonged to Bill and Rachel Kenyon, and attracted more sponsor money than some of the human walkers. (K.F.*)

In the year 1507, the restrictive settlement laws on the ancient Forest of Rossendale were relaxed. The village of Newchurch grew up around the "kirk" of 1511, which served the dual purpose of a place of worship for the new inhabitants and a landmark for travellers. Newchurch became a centre of the thriving woollen industry in the 1700s, and even as late as 1848, the railway station in Waterfoot was designated as "Newchurch". The huddled village seen here retained its character until the "slum" clearance programme of the 1960s. In the foreground is Boothfold, "Turnpike" curves round on the right and the roof of Thistlemount House is just visible in the trees, centre. (R.C.T.)

A stone church replaced one of wood and thatch in 1561, and the Elizabethan date stone still survives, as do the hexagonal pillars under the gallery. The present church was built in 1826, with a chancel added in 1896. It has outlived and absorbed later parishes, and is now known as St. Nicholas with St John, (formerly at Cloughfold) recently taking over St. James, Waterfoot and St. Michael's at Lumb. The old school is on the left. (R.C.T.)

The oldest surviving houses are on Old Street, behind the church, and were clearly once a typical local "hall house" of the late 16th century. It became divided into cottages as the working population increased and its owners moved up in the world, probably in the mid 1700s. As one of Rossendale's earliest Listed buildings, it escaped the demolition of the greater part of the village. This drawing is by Celia Lord, who in July 2003 still lives next door. (Celia Lord*.)

The old Mansion House, home of the Hargreaves family and later the Vicarage, was not so lucky, being one of the most serious architectural losses in the area. Henry Hargreaves, born in 1741, kept a diary which still exists, and gives a wonderful picture of his life in Rossendale in 1760. Henry and his son George both became solicitors in Waterfoot, playing a major part in the development of the Industrial Revolution in the area. The date stone of 1720 can be seen at Whitaker Park. (J.D.*)

The top of Old Street as demolition began to bite into the close-knit fabric of the village. The huddle round the church was not only economic in land use, but provided warmth and shelter on the windy hillside. (J.D.*)

The bottom of Old Street, which once linked up to the lane still known as "Bridleway". The two were cut across in the 1820s by the new Turnpike road, a name that has also been retained. Facing back up the street is the gable of the "Volunteers" hotel, built on the junction of the two routes and named after the militia raised by Colonel Munn of Thistlemount House. (J.D.*)

Kirk Fair was held in June, originating as a cattle market but later becoming a Show with displays and entertainments. It has long since gone, but the routine cattle sales survived until the turn of the 19th century, as shown in this picture of the Square, opposite the Boar's Head, with Back Street behind. (R.C.T.)

A view up Back Street in the 1960s, when the house seen behind the cattle had already gone, and those on the right are awaiting demolition. (J.D.*)

Another view of Back Street with three-storey Georgian town houses shows the ambition of Newchurch in the 1700s, although at sometime even the top floors of these houses may have been used for weaving. It was proposed to set up a Cloth Market here in the 1760s, but merchants continued to travel further afield to Rochdale, Colne and Halifax, so Newchurch never acheived its full potential. (R.C.T.)

Oddfellows Hall in Church Street. The "Oddfellows" were a benevolent society who provided an early form of insurance cover for thrifty working class people. In many towns and villages they erected Assembly Rooms which could be used for secular meetings and visiting speakers. (J.D.*)

The Turnpike road of the 1820s attracted the building of loomshops, some with accommodation for workers on the ground floor. By this time, weavers were supplied with ready-prepared beams by the spinning mills whose owners often built the loomshops themselves in the form of long terraces, but enterprising individuals still built their own in the midst. (J.D.*)

Above left: Dark Lane was originally a footpath down to Holt Mill. Buildings grew up around its junction with Church Street, including the one (left) known as the Farm, although this three storey block seems purpose built for hand-loom weaving. (J.D.*) *Above right:* Most of the houses on Church Street had loom accommodation, and outdoor stairs (these are behind no. 39) were for carrying the beams from the mill to the top floors – they were far too large to go round narrow corners inside. This also explains the absence of any stair rails, which does not appear to have been seen as a hazard either to the weavers or the child who has left her doll after playing there in the early 1960s. (J.D.*) *Below:* The old "Lock-up," next to the Farm, was probably the "dungeon" constructed following a decree of "November ye 11th, 1788 " after a "publick meeting" signed by " J. Shorrock, Jno. Hargreaves, Lawce. Ormerod, (High Constable) and 14 others." (J.D.*)

The "Boar's Head" in the Square bears a datestone of 1674, but the present building seems more mid 18th century. The name could go back to the early days of the Forest clearances. The "Blue Bell" behind the church is a 19th century building. The "Boar's Head" and block of shops are now all that remains of Church Street, the two centre shops, with remains of bow windows, being Listed. (J.D.*)

An unusually strong gale in September 1978 caused the spectacular collapse of the roof of the "Boar's Head." The extension to the back was also severely damaged. It was re-built with a modern tiled roof, but the walls have been cleaned back to stone after many years under various colours of paint. (R.C.T.)

Church Street in 1964; a mixture of houses and workshops. It is a great pity that these buildings were not even recorded, let alone preserved. These were the days before Conservation Areas and Rossendale was not considered to have any history or tourist potential. The loss of Newchurch still rankles with local people who knew and loved it. (J.D.*)

John Taylor Wright and his wife Jane lived at 51 Church Street in the 1890s and their daughter Nellie, with her husband Heyes Hoyle, lived there until just before the 1960s demolition. John was a felt worker, and a bell ringer at St. Nicholas'. The seven daughters are (back) Nellie, Emma, Fanny and Ada; (front), Annie, Lizzie and Lena. (Phyllis Howarth)

The sad sight of Church Street, abandoned in the 1960s. The demolition was piecemeal and untidy, which hurt every bit as much as the loss itself. (J.D.*)

Above: The same site with clearance complete, the top of Turnpike and Old Street facing the remains of the Square. (Clarence Hoyle*)

Left: After road widening, Council houses were built on the sites compulsorily purchased for demolition. These are roughly in the area between Church Street and Back Street on pages 122 and 126. (J.D.*)

Before the loss of the village houses, the population of Newchurch was boosted by the building of Staghills estate in the 1950s, which has enabled the local chapels, churches and schools to survive. However, the attendance at St. Nicholas' Sunday School class, seen here in 1959, would be the envy of any one of them today. (R.C.S.)

In St. Nicholas' churchyard is the grave of "Old 'Thu," Methusalah Yates, who died in February 1864. He was a huntsman for 50 years, twenty five of them with the Rossendale Hunt. The harrier has kept his guard ever since, and in 2003 was given Grade Two Star Listed building status. (K.F.*)

Newchurch Unitarians were a major group in the village with origins as "Cookites," followers of a preacher named Cook in the early 1800s, before becoming part of the Unitarian mainstream. Records of the church have recently been saved, catalogued and deposited at Lancashire County Records office, including this picture of Walking Day outside the church on Turnpike in July 1901. (R.G.)

Competitors from Newchurch and Rawtenstall Unitarian Sunday Schools with the "Shield" they won at the North East Lancashire Arts and Crfts exhibition at Colne, in an undated picture from the 1930s. The Pastor was W. Millar of Raby Street, Rawtenstall. (R.C.T.)

Left: Newchurch Grammar School had its origins in an endowment by John Kershaw in 1701. It stood "a little below the village" and was rebuilt,in 1829-30 at the junction of Bridleway and the then new Turnpike. Entry for pupils was by scholarship only until the education reforms of the early 1900s, after which it was completely replaced in 1913 by Bacup and Rawtenstall Secondary (later Grammar) School at Waterfoot. Tom Watson, pictured on page 14, was one of its last students. The building was demolished in the 1980s and is now the site of a house. (K.F.*)

Below: Newchurch Methodists trace their origins back to 1744 at Millar Barn Lane, Waterfoot, the site opposite the Old Grammar School by the side of Bridleway and Turnpike being first used in 1806. This building served the congregation from 1971 until 1950. It had a large Sunday School behind, which has been used for used for worship ever since. (R.C.T.)

Ashlands was the home of "Dickie Deb's," Richard Ashworth of the Longholme feltworks that became the site of "Asda." Set back from Turnpike, behind a richly carved stone wall, it is one of the most beautiful of all Rossendale's mill owner's mansions. It is now a nursing home, and retains most of its original interior, the main drawing room cieling being painted with panels of playful cherubs. (J.D.*)

Staghills House was built by yet another Richard Ashworth, whose full ambitious plan never materialised. It came nowhere near the same standard as the exquisite little gate house that still stands on Bacup Road, and only just survived the 1940s as a dangerous ruin before the 1950s Council housing estate was built on the site and grounds. (R.C.T.)

Another fine Newchurch house, Heightside, is also now a Nursing home, although for many years it was the headquarters of the European Christian Mission, with printing works in the former stables. It was the home of Colonel Bolton, associated with the formation of the National Coal Board in 1948. This picture was taken before the alterations of the 1980s, and shows the central (Listed) Georgian house with its Victorian wing behind, left, and single storey billiards room, right. (K.F.*)

The interior of Heightside remained very much the same until the Mission left in the early '80s. This is one of the drawing rooms in the Victorian wing with homely fittings of the 1930s, from an undated photograph. (R.C.T.)

Rose Cottage was the summer house to Heightside, an idyllic retreat with views over the Valley. In the midst of the wooded hillside, it had a formerly laid-out garden with rose-covered pergolas and a lily pond. (R.C.T.)

No one has ever given a proper explanation of the circle of stones that crown the brow of the hill at Seat Naze. Its format suggests a sheep fold, but its exposed position makes this questionable. Whatever its original purpose, it has long been a focal point for a walk up the hill from Newchurch, and a view point for the landscape for miles around. (J.D.*)

Rossendale United are based at Newchurch, their ground being just off Dark Lane. In 1926-27 and 1928-29 they won the championship of the Lancashire Combination and are seen here returning with the Cup in 1927. They were met at the Borough Boundary by the Mayor, Councillor Peter Trickett, and crowds of people cheered them through the streets to Waterfoot. (R.C.T.)

Once again champions, this time of the Cheshire League in 1970-71. Back row, Manager L. Rigby, Subs. W. Roberts and C. Wroth, R. Wilkinson, D.Wild, Goalkeeper J. Wood, Dennis Crompton, E Bichall, G. Barker, T. Unsworth, and Trainer T. Nuttall. Front, Jim Hommell (Sub.), Dave Crompton, B. Greenon, Captian Bob Woods, J. Pearson, P. Bourne, K. Fletcher. (David Howarth)

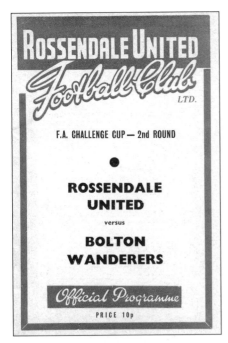

1971 was a good year for the Club; they won through to the First Round proper of the F.A.Cup when they defeated Altrincham at Dark Lane (which lived up to its name due to a floodlight controversy) and went on to meet Bolton Wanderers in Round Two, playing at Bury's Gigg Lane but were defeated 4-1. (David Howarth)

One of Rossendale United's most popular characters has been goalkeeper Steve Hodgson, who is currently a Club Director and a regular organiser of local charitable events. Here (right) he presents DErek Hutchinson with a cheque from the Players for Ball Advertising. (David Howarth)

2001 and yet another Championship, this time of the Bass North West Counties League, which they won at Flixton. (David Howarth)

Malcolm Lord receives a certificate from Mayor Jimmy Grogan after completeing a Sponsored swim to raise funds for Rossendale United's new stand in 2001. Malcolm is a switchboard operator at the Town Hall. (David Howarth)

Rawtenstall finally got its own swimming pool just before local government reorganisation in 1974, sited at the Marl Pits Sports Centre on Newchurch Road. There are many swimming enthusiasts in the valley, and Marl Pits has proved a versatile pool for both play and sport. (Ross. Borough Council)

Left: Rawtenstall's sports centre was created at Marl Pits, from land re-claimed from the Borough's refuse tip. Construction involved moving 110,000 tons of soil and laying eight miles of drainage pipe. The site originally occupied twenty seven acres on four graded levels, providing an athletics track, football and rugby pitches. The opening ceremony ws on September 6th 1969. (Lancashire Life)

Right: Teacher Eddie Roberts (right) became captain of the new athletic Club, seen here with collegue Alan Taylor. (Lancashire Life)

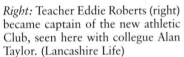

Left: The superior conditions at Marl Pits attracted schools from all over the valley for Sports Days. The girls here are from Bacup and Rawtenstall Grammar School in 1980. (K.F.*)

Rawtenstall Cricket Club won the Lancashire League title in 1927 with 41 points, having only lost one match all season. The Cup was presented by Mr. Barlow, League Secretary, to Club Captain G.R. Holt. (R.C.T.)

The Worswick Memorial Ground was donated by the family in 1955, and has banks of south facing terraces. The Club has a dedicated local following, and some matches between Valley teams become quite lively occasions. (K.F.*)

Rawtenstall First Eleven in 1977. Bert Hanson, with beard on the right, is now Chairman of the Lancashire League and Malcolm Ashton, far left, is now full-time England analyst. Next to him is Team Manager Roger Medlock, and centre front Team Captain Peter Wood. (Peter Wood)

August 2003 saw the end of a thirteen year gap in the club's trophy trail. They won the Lancashire League's "knock-out" competition for the Worseley Cup, and in fine style with an innings of 223 for 7 before scuttling East Lancs for 89 all out. (David Dawson*)

Peter Wood leaves the ground as he retires from the game in 1996, having started his career at Rawtenstall at the age of 12 in 1962. Peter established a Lancashire League record for the highest number of runs accumulated - 14, 951, including 11 centuries and 99 "50s" and achieving the record number of runs in a season of 1227 at an average of 53.35. (Peter Wood)

In 1969, a survey initiated by Tony Greenwood for "New Life in Old Towns" suggested that an artificial Ski-slope be added to the facilities at Marl Pits. The terrain in the unused part of Whitaker Park proved to be better suited to the task and it quickly became remarkably popular. The short slope seen here in the early 1970s was soon extended up the hill, making it for many years the longest artificial slope in England. (K.F.*)

Youngsters queue for the drag lift who would probably never have had any other opportunity to experience skiing. The slope, although now surpassed in length by others, is still one of Rossendale's main visitor attractions. (K.F.*)

Chapter 11 – Waterfoot

The meeting-place of the Irwell and two of its main tributaries, the brooks of Cowpe and Whitewell, is aptly named Waterfoot. It did not become a place in its own right until the mid 1800s, when the railway arrived (1848) and the parish of St. James' was formed from Newchurch, Tunstead and Spotland (1865). Its place in the heart of Rossendale's hills comes out very clearly in this picture. (R.G.)

Mill End, where the "Turnpike" to Newchurch went over the river to Boothfold, and was later crossed by Burnley Road East. The chimney is at Sir. H.W.Trickett's Gaghills shoe factory, and the tall gable to the right is Bethel Baptist church, which was supported in the early 1900s by Sir Henry himself. (R.C.T.)

Warth Road was the main route along the bottom of the valley towards Rawtenstall before the present A681 was constructed in the 1820s. Warth House was an elegant dwelling of the late 18th century, complete with shell porch, probably financed out of the new wealth of the early industrial revolution. (R.C.T.)

The 1960s re-vamp of Warth House shows how little our local history counted for at that time. Yet even this has now been demolished as Warth Road is considered part of a possible Waterfoot by-pass. (R.C.T.)

The Kings Cinema, well past its "sell-by" date when this picture was taken in 1962, was the venue for many of Trickett's Choral Society concerts in the 1920s and later gave hundreds of local kids their Saturday matinee thrills with Batman, Buck Rogers and a host of favourite cowboys. (J.D.*)

Above: Trickett's Arcade was built by Sir Henry Whittaker Trickett, five times Mayor of Rawtenstall, in 1899 in order to make Waterfoot a major shopping centre. It incorporates an inner area, originally accessed by a gate on the front corner as well as at each side, two outer rows of shops, and could generate its own electricity. At present very much under-used, it has enormous potential, and was Listed as a building of architectural importance in 1997. (K.F.*)

Left: Sir Henry died in 1913 and a memorial clock was erected on the corner of the Arcade between Bacup Road and Burnley Road East. It was unveiled on June 13th 1914 by Rossendale's M.P. Lewis Harcourt. For a long time the responsiblity of winding it up fell to the tenant of the first floor corner flat. (R.C.T.)

Left: After the second world war, refugees came to the valley from Eastern Europe, and most settled quite happily into the old terraced streets. The lady here is Jari Manzewitch , with Michael Manzewitch (left) and nephew Boris Averchenko. The Averchenkos were Ukranian, and lived at 628 Bacup Road. The picture was taken in Spring Garden Street, between the Moulders' Arms and Stotts Buildings in the mid 1950s. (R.G.)

Below: 630 Bacup Road was a pork butchers in 1891, "Hudson's Dining Rooms" in 1900, a physiotherapist's consulting rooms in the 1920s and Walter and Nora Horne's shoe shop in the 1950s. It was converted to the Copper Kettle Snack Bar by Isaac Bleazard from Cowpe in 1955, and bought by Patrick Joseph Maxwell and his wife Winifred in 1962. Customers sat up to the high counter on tall stools, and it was popular for many years. (R.G.)

Many of the houses and shops in central Waterfoot are built on the very edge of the river banks, and access by bridges to the backs of Bacup Road over the Irwell gave this part the nick-name "Little Venice." Cowpe Brook joins the Irwell from the right just before the Bridge. (R.C.T.)

A closer picture of Baron Fold, also on the left above, just before demolition about 1960. A very distinctive and unique "loomshop", the side on the right was originally a two-storey building with a multi-windowed top floor workshop added around 1770 to cash in on the booming woollen trade. The two-storey block has more domestic proportions but the upper floors could also have held looms. (R.C.T.)

Waterfoot station, looking towards Bacup. The track crossed Cowpe Road by bridge and the platforms were at first -floor level behind the booking office on Bacup Road, accessed by a rickety wooden stair. In this picture, taken about 1960, the two tunnels through the Glen are just visible in the centre distance. (R.C.T.)

Waterfoot Station looking west, towards Rawtenstall. The tall chimney on the right is at the back of the Royal Hotel, where once the manufacturers from the Whitewell Valley met and entertained potential customers arriving by train from far and wide. Baron Fold is on the right of the track in the mid distance. (R.C.T.)

Right: Bacup and Rawtenstall Secondary School, the successor to Newchurch Grammar, was opened at Glen Road, Waterfoot on Sepember 13th 1913. It took over two years to build at a cost of over £26,000, the architect being Mr. Littler of Lancashire County Council. It did not become known as the Grammar School again until 1928. (R.C.T.)

Above left: An early B.R.S.S. Magazine – "Daphne" is from the Greek "Laurel" - only given to the best. Yet the content has more amusing than serious selections of work, plus articles on fund raising for the War effort and a girls' hockey match in Burnley, where they travelled on a "conveyance" called "The Lily," which had to stop at an Inn on the way back to allow the driver to get a candle for his lamp. (R.C.T.) *Above right:* Ten years later, the magazine has up-dated in name, and style with an Art Deco cover by the Art Master, Mr. Barker. The school's year had included visits by a lecturer on Flemish art and the Halle Orchestra. (R.C.T.)

In contrast to the staid opening ceremony, the entrance stairs in 1985 hold a group on "non-uniform day" - for pupils, but not for staff, who swopped places. (Shirley Richmond)

The school has always had both boys and girls, taught in mixed classes, although there have been separate men's and women's staff rooms for most of its life. In this 1930s picture, girls seem to be kept strictly to uniform, whilst boys have more freedom. (R.G.)

Staff of B.R.G.S., October 1952. To teach at B.R.G.S. was a way of life rather than a job, many staff staying for most of their whole career. This group from 1952 are remembered by many people in the Valley and beyond. At the top; Mr. Proctor and Mr. Ralph Collinson; next row Mr. Jack Cawthorne, Mrs. Chedzoy, Mr. Blainey, Miss Brown, Mr. Pell, Miss Newall and Mr. Jack Bridge. Third row, Mrs. Collinson, Miss Hammer, Miss Reece, Miss Jean Macleroy, Mrs. Elizabeth Culley, Miss Mary Dodds, Mr. Niel Maclean, Mr. Trevor Park, Mr. Humpston, Mr. Eric Ward and Mr. Frank Harding. Front row, Mrs. Lonsdale, Mrs. Ebden, Miss Margaret Moore, Miss Dorothy Moore, Deputy Headmistress Miss Phyllis Irene Greenwood, Headmaster Mr. William Copley, , Mr. Duthie, Mr. Ebden, Mr. Fielden and Mr. Milton Ormerod. (J.W.)

With its informal lay-out, the main Art Room was always the most relaxed place in the school, but turned out some excellent students, including fashion designer Betty Jackson. (K.F.)

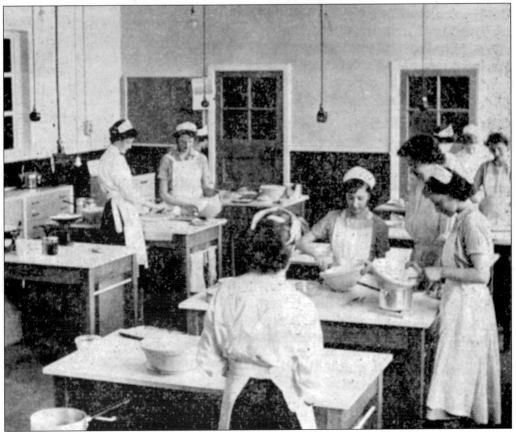

Domestic Science was an important subject when the school was built in 1913, and the room was equipped to the best standards of the time. This group of girls were being taught by Miss Connie Dracup in 1958, wearing caps and aprons they had made themselves in needlework classes. (K.F.)

In January 1960 the school broke new ground and ambitiously produced Benjamin Brittain's Opera "Noye's Fludde", the first time in public after its debut at Aldeborough. Skilfully directed by music master Michael Nuttall, an orchestra of seventy and cast of another thirty turned out an unforgettable performance, using the whole hall and involving the audience. The resonant "voice of God" from the balcony above was provided by John (Jack) Nicholls, who later became Bishop of Lancaster and currently of Sheffield. (K.F.)

Jack Nicholls was featured in the national Press as "Britain's only Bearded Schoolboy" when he took the part of Raguel in the 1961 production of "Tobias and the Angel" (third from right, standing). The many talented actors at B.R.G.S. developed their skills in fourth (later third) year form drama competitions, introduced by English master Mr. E.J. (Pop) Williams. (K.F.)

Speech day at B.R.G.S., 1981. Before the formation of the Borough of Rossendale in 1974, the Mayors of Rawtenstall and Bacup attended the Speech days, but pictured here are Rossendale's Vernon Smith and his wife Marjorie, with councillor Bernard Forkin of Bury, reflecting the widening catchment area. Rawtenstall's Town Clerk in wig, is Mr. William Wolfe, and Headmaster Phillip Clark delivers the address. Guest speaker was Dr. Michael Pilling, M.A. PhD., tutor for admissions at Jesus College Oxford and a former B.R.G.S. pupil. (Kathleen Gowers)

In July 1991 Headmaster Martyn Morris (right) said goodbye to three long serving members of staff, Shirley Richmond, Ken Holgate, and, shaking hands, Gordon Phillips, who came in 1956. B.R.G.S. in 1989 took Grant Maintained status, and is still a selective Grammar School. (Shirley Richmond)

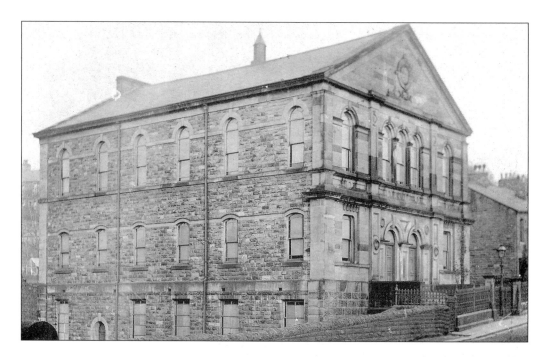

Above: Waterfoot had its own fair share of religious establishments, now mainly memories. "Bethesda" (Methodists) stood on Ashworth Road and is now the site of new housing. (R.C.T.)

Right: In the 1950s there was a flourishing youth group, seen here on the 75th anniversary in 1953, but soon like many others to be lost to more modern attractions. (R. Mus.)

Right: Members leave the closing service in March 1957. Those named in this picture are Colin and Margaret Everett (behind the lady third from left on the front row) and Harry Hill, in overcoat, right. (R. Mus.)

Bethel Baptists, on Burnley Road East, is said to have started with a Congregation of six in 1854, and ended, again with six, in November 1994. This unusual Chapel, built in 1869, featured an open Baptistry, on the platform, right, and stained glass windows bearing the monogram of slipper "King" Henry Trickett. This picture was taken only minutes before the removal men came to clear the furniture, some of which is now in Whitaker Park Museum. (K.F.*)

Bethel Baptist Choir 1934/35. Concerts were the thing, and the Choir Revue a white tie occasion. This group includes choir master Ronald Ashworth (fifth from left, seated), and Alec Richards, dancing master, (seventh left), as well as members of the Tomlinson, Taylor and Beardsworth families. (Jennifer Crews.)

Waterfoot Conservative Club has also been a major social centre for many years, celebrating its centenary in 1989. It began as Newchurch and District Working Men's Conservative Association, whose billiards team won the Rossendale Conservative Club League in 1923-24. Far right on the back row is George Henry Birtwistle , ex Councillor, teacher at Cowpe Sunday School and Club Treasurer. To his right is Billy Feber, who worked at Trickett's Gaghills Mill for over fifty years. (R.G.)

Rossendale M.P. David (now Sir David) Trippier at the centenary celebrations with the Club Committee. (R.G.)

Waterfoot County Primary School is a characterful building of the early 1900s on Thornfield Avenue, its playground tucked away between a wooded bank and the River Whitewell. This group of the 1920s shows evidence of the raising of the school leaving age; a few years earlier most of the tall boys at the back would have gone into the mills as "part timers". (R.G.)

A contrasting group from April 1989, joining in a Civic clean-up. With Deputy Head Dave Prisnall, they filled ten bags with litter for the "Spring Clean" effort. (R.C.T.)

Trickett's was not the only shoe factory in Waterfoot; on Burnley Road East was Hirsts, which continued in business until the late 1990s. Seen here in May 1996, an operative matches a shoe upper to the sole as part of the lasting process. (K.F.*)

Rawtenstall Civic Society awarded its 1994 "Best Shop Front" certificate to the the chemists at 717 Bacup Road, now a picture framing shop, but still with its beautifully kept original facade. The judge on this occasion was Ian Goldthorpe, Rossendale's former Chief Planning Officer, here making the presentation with his wife Mary in the foreground. (K.F.*)

The Rossendale players were formed in 1936 from a W.E.A. Arts group. Mainly based in Waterfoot, they now have their "Millenium Theatre" in the old Bethel Baptist Lecture Hall. Here, they celebrate the 50th production, "The Man Who Came To Dinner," at the Conservative Club in May 1950. (R.G.)

The first production was "The Circle", performed again in 2000. In front, left to right, Maureen Jackson, Carol Anne Connelly, Susannah Cooper; behind, left to right, Emmeline Smith, Roy Preston, Robin Grffiths, Geoffrey Collinge, Ward Croasdale and Tony Harris. Director was Stanley Whittaker. (Stanley Whittaker)

A keen member and publicity agent for the players was George, one of the musical Holt family of Waterfoot. The Humber car was bought in the 1920s to carry pianos supplied by their shop on the corner of Wood Lea and Burnley Road East, and later made regular appearances in parades and carnivals until the 1990s. This outing was to promote the Players' production of "Ring Round the Moon" in 1959, and was taken just off Bacup Road in Rawtenstall, with Cawl Terrace Co-op in the background. Left to right are Clarence (Larry) Roberts, Patricia Kay, Diana Pilling, Tom Rawstron, George Holt and Alan Ratcliffe. (R.C.T.)

"Ring Round the Moon" – the production, on stage - left to right, Fred Howarth, Diana Pilling, Clarence Roberts, Patricia Kay, Maureen Whitford, Muriel West, Olwen Stansfield, Alan Hough, Margaret Ainscow, Tom Rawstron and Stanley Whittaker, directed by Margaret Cropper. (Stanley Whitaker)

In 1989 and the early 1990s Waterfoot had an annual "Medieval Day" fair, with stalls, floats, and music. This reconstruction of a Castle aboard one of J.F. Riley's wagons was complete with banqueting hall and pillory. (J. Hince)

Jim and Anthony Hince of Taylor's Decorators hoped to bring the town out of the dark ages with a special paint sale, inspired by the monks of Stanlaw (and later Whalley) Abbey who cultivated the area in the 13th century. (J. Hince)

St. James' Walking day, August 1970, with Janet Smith as Rose Queen. Under the church spire, on the far left, the belfry held what was said to be the best peal of bells in Rossendale, which were transferred to Sefton after closure in November 1998.

In the centre of the three storey buildings was Edgar Lord's Plumbers, a firm which supplied glass, lead, piping and fittings to houses and businesses throughout the Valley, and whose files now belong to Rossendale Civic Trust. (Mary Smith)

Choir of St. James' Church, 1960s. On the left is Father Trevor Richardson, who later resigned in protest at the Church of England's decision to ordain women priests. Centre back is Dennis Black, former Rawtenstall Borough Engineer and Surveyor, and head choir boy on the left of the second row is Tim Nuttall, now of Rossendale Borough Council's Tourist Office. David Worsley, on the right of the row next to the back, completed 60 years service with the choir (1937 - 1997). He remembers - "There used to be dances that were packed out and you had to get tickets in advance. The church pantomimes were the same. We had choir trips, concerts and performed cantatas and Messiah." St. James' closed in November 1998, and has been converted to offices and flats. (David Worsley)

Chapter 12 – Whitewell Valley

Above: The narrow valley of the River Whitewell, from its origin on the moors to its junction with the Irwell, was home to a large number of small, independent mills of very early date, many of them at first waterpowered. Although some of these have been lost quite recently, many do survive, as can be seen in this view of 1999 from behind "Ashlands", and the valley is a happy hunting ground for industrial archaeologists. (K. F.*)

Left: Lambert Howarths, another shoe factory, seen just before its demolition. In front is the new Whitewell Valley Community Centre, which was built on the site of the old school which served this part of the valley for both junior and secondary education until the 1930s. The chimney carries the firm's centenary marker. (K. F. *)

Above: Variety was the keynote to the industries of the Whitewell Valley. Bownesses, on Shawclough Road, was one of several Rossendale mineral water firms, the soft spring water allowing a perfect blend with the flavours. Originally a waterpowered woollen mill, Bownesses was burnt down in August 1989 and is now replaced with modern units. This picture was taken in August 1976. (K.F.*)

Right: Local breweries also benefitted from the good water, and amongst them was Baxters of Waterfoot, this stone bottle dating from the early 20th century (R.C.T.)

Below: Bownesses also produced boiled sweets as a spin-off from the mineral water business. Dating from the 1950s at latest, this humble toffee paper is a very rare survivor. Cellophane paper was produced in Bury, so it was a typical example of local industries traditionally working together. (R.C.T.)

Left: Shawclough once had three mills all powered from the same tributary of the Whitewell. The stonework in the foreground is the remains of a waterwheel pit, with the stream running on into Jack Lodge behind ready to power the next one. The square chimneys belonged to very early steam engines, which at first were used to supplement the water power when streams were low in summer. (K.F.*)

Below: Shawclough attracts students of the Industrial Revolution from far and wide, but this local group made a special study of remaining Rossendale chimneys in 1990, including production of a video, hoping to attract wider interest in the area's rich heritage. (K.F.*)

Grime Bridge Colliery, on the edge of the moors near the head of the valley, was one of several small suppliers to local mills. Rossendale had no large coal mines; they were mainly shallow or open cast, and sited towards the north and east of the area. Grime Bridge was one of the few in the Borough of Rawtenstall, and was by far the last one in production, continuing until fairly recently. This group was photographed there in the much more productive days of the 1920s. (R.G.)

Salem Chapel (Methodist) was at the bottom of Shawclough Road, and closed in the 1960s, becoming a works for knives for the shoe industry process known as "clicking". This Sunday School walk down Burnley Road East is undated but must be from the 1950s. The houses behind were demolished in the 1960s slum clearances. (J.D.)

Left: Land was at a premium in the Whitewell Valley, and houses often perched on narrow hillside ledges. The lack of proper water and drainage facilities led to some being abandoned as the 20th century wore on. These remains were pictured at Higher Scout in 1964. (J.D.*)

Right: St. Anne's Primary School at Edgeside also makes use of the steep valley sides with a tiered playground. This is another of the area's quiet, efficient traditional schools which still have a village atmosphere. (St. Annes)

Left: This was one of the last of the real Lancashire Valleys and until recently Burnley Road East did not carry much traffic. Despite the amount of industry on the valley floor, there is good farmland on the hilltops, and milk was delivered by horse drawn floats until well within living memory. This pony and trap were at Lower Scout in 1964. (J.D.*)

In Whitewell Bottom in 1961 it was still possible to walk down the middle of the road without much danger. This is the junction of Burnley Road East and Hightown road, Hightown being a late example of a terrace on the narrow hillside and the roadside terraces ending in corner shops. (J.D.*)

These are genuine "back-to-back" houses, each with a tiny kitchen window by one side of the door, the larger one to the other side lighting the living room. The adjoining houses behind would be a mirror image. It was a lack of through ventilation that led this type of dwelling to fail the health regulations of the 1950s, although in practice the chimneys with an open fire created an efficient enough air circulation, and "knocking through" produced a good sized family home. The sturdy construction of this particular row did in fact ensure its survival . (R.C.T.)

In the 1960s this new Council housing estate at Brockclough won a prestigeous National Award, and looked like a blue-print for the rest of the area, especially the Whitewell Valley, to follow. It proved to be a one-off, and the "slum" clearances were not as drastic here as elsewhere, leaving a legacy of different types of terraced houses along Burnley Road East that could well repay closer study. (K.F.)

The last block of houses before Burnley Road East stretches over the moor is Graver Weir Terrace, a block of back-to-backs with what were once called "cellar dwellings" beneath, rather like Rawtenstall's Ormerod Street. They were built by the nearby mill-owner for his workers about 1854. In the 1980s, the residents, who had opened up the "cellars" as utility rooms, fought and won the battle for preservation, enisting the help of architect Rod Hackney. The result was the creation of spacious family houses with a landscaped communal garden. (K.F.*)

An undated picture of workers and staff at Forest Mill. Small, locally run factories survived in the Whitewell Valley longer than anywhere else in Rossendale. Workers were loyal and proud and products were usually for specialist markets before the days of cheap competiton from abroad. (J.D.)

Albert Works at Whitewell Bottom was one of the biggest factories in the Whitewell Valley, occupying both sides of the road below Rock Bridge. Linking the premises, this purely artificial structure was built as a Coronation Arch in 1953, but remained in position for some time afterwards, becoming one of the most memorable features of the area. (J.D.)

Albert Works produced felt, a branch of the woollen industry, and the single storey sheds and settling beds took up rare flat land in a bend of the river. Felt was used for many purposes in industry as well as furnishing, including local production of paper and slippers. (R.C.T.)

One of the finishing processes, with the material under keen inspection. When Albert Works was demolished, the land between the road and the river was considered unsuitable for re-building, and the site of the sheds in these two pictures is left empty. A small, well-designed development, Rock Bridge Fold, overlooks the landscaped grassy space from the other side of the river. (R.C.T.)

By the 1840s, the population of the Whitewell Valley was enough to merit a new church; it was built in 1848 by the architect James Clarke in the Romanesque rather than the then popular Gothic style, in a dramatic setting atop a prominent hill. St. Michaels became embroiled in the High versus Low Church arguments in the 1920s, and the disagreements between a large proportion of its congregation and the Vicar, Theophilus Caleb, made national news. (J.D.)

St. Michael's Sunday School, in the 1970s, was still playing an active role in the community, children coming in from the scatttered farms. As the church building fell into disrepair, they met in the nearby home of John and Marjorie Walsh. (M. Walsh)

Above: St. Michael's Walking Day, early 1970s. Led by John Walsh, the vicar, Rev. Keith Harrison flanked by Church Wardens Hilda Haworth and James Schofield, are seen at Lumb Corner, where the road takes a hairpin bend round the foot of the church bank. Accompanying the parade is Water Brass Band, and behind them in the background the former Lumb School. (M. Walsh)

The east end of the church was abandoned in the 1970s, the nave being the only part kept in use, and the congregation managed to stay in existance until the early 1990s. The Chancel, seen in its full glory above right, had become a ruin and upkeep proved too much (right). The final redundancy notice was issued in May 2003, by which time plans had been accepted for conversion to a large, well designed house, hopefully securing the future of this unusual building. (K.F.*)

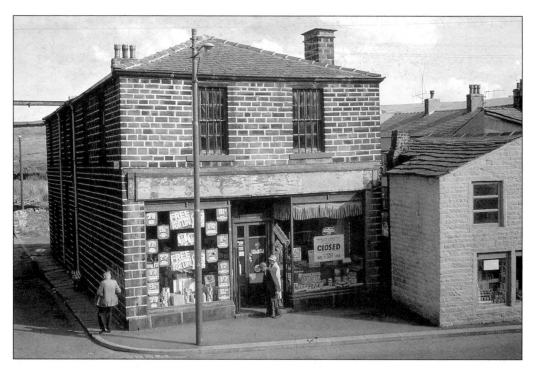

Closure of Water Co-op, September 1965. For many years the village of Water had several shops, including a butchers, confectioners and newsagents, as well as this branch of the Co-op, all around the junction with Burnley Road East and Dean Lane, once a well used route over the moors to Bacup. The Co-op building survived and is now the one central Village Store. (J.D.*)

Despite being such a small and semi-rural area, Water village at the top of the Whitewell Valley has a large and well-known brass band. Formed in 1866, Water Prize Band was the successor to the musical traditions of the local chapels, amongst whose "orchestras" members had played. The name "Prize" was a reference to the competitions entered in the 1890s and early 1900s, including Crystal Palace in 1912 when they took a cabin trunk of sandwiches for food on the train. But their winnings were modest, and they soon became simply "Water Band", closely associated with the village community, probably a factor that has contributed to their long survival. Some of its recent successes were between 1975 and 1985, to which many of the members in this picture from 1991 contributed. (Alan Cropper)

Chapter 13 – People who set the pace and make the place

Fred Tomlinson, Male Voice Choir leader, lived at 41 Beech Street, where he and his wife May brought up their talented family, Freda, Ernest, Fred junior and James. All followed in their father's musical footsteps and went to Manchester Cathedral Choir School. Here, Fred and May set off from Beech Street with the children for a picnic on the slopes of Cribden. (F. T.)

Ernest Tomlinson has become one of Britain's most popular composers of light music, his best known piece probably being "Little Serenade". In recent years Ernest has been busy in Bratislava conducting new, live orchestral recordings of the classics for the "Naxos" C.D. label. (F.T.)

As May Culpan, May Tomlinson started the first Girl Guides at St. Mary's, seen here in 1915, as the 77th Manchester group. As other Rossendale companies were formed, and the district came into its own, they became the 1st Rossendale Guides in 1923. On this picture in St. Mary's school yard, May is on the right of the three leaders, the leader on the left being Nan Hutchinson.(F.T.)

In the spring of 1974, a tree was planted in St. Mary,s churchyard in memory of Nan Hutchinson by the youngest Guide and youngest Brownie. The Tomlinsons had by then moved into the Culpan family home at Derby Terrace, and May watches over the railings on the right, next to Mrs. Robinson of Crawshawbooth; Freda is in the doorway and Fred on her left. This house has been in the ownership of the Culpan family since it was built and Freda still lives there in 2003. (F.T.)

In 1977, Beech Street was one of the many in Rawtenstall to hold a party for the Queen's Silver Jubilee. This neighbour-hood is one where some residents have stayed for many years, and the party gave an opportunity for old and new of all ages to get together. (K.F.*)

The "Piggy Back" race was one of several which took up the whole street and brought out the community spirit. The view over the town behind includes Higher Mill chimney and the distant hills towards Bacup. (K.F.*)

Jack Trickett and Austin Whipp, both teachers at B.R.G.S., carved the coat-of-arms for Rawtenstall Council Chamber in 1969. It still hangs in the present Town Hall. (K.F.)

The coat-of-arms is a 2ft 6ins square of mahogany, left in its natural wood finish. The stags, wolf and squirrel refer to the Old Forest of Rossendale: the cows and cotton bales to later settlement – a rare use of the cow in heraldry. (K.F.)

One of Rawtenstall's characters is road-sweeper Colin Hyland. No mechanical device is as meticulous as Colin was. As well as being a stalwart supporter of Rawtenstall cricket club, Colin has been a self-appointed Mayor's attendant for many years, giving support to many local charitable events. (R.C.T.)

Jon Elliott (left) became Borough Librarian and Museum Curator in 1958, both then run by Rawtenstall corporation. Jon was instrumental in getting the first listed buildings in the town in 1963, and starting the Arts and Antiquities Society from which grew the Civic Society and the Friends of the Museum. Just before take-over by Lancashire County Council in 1974, Rawtenstall Library came second in a national survey of best local libraries. Jon is seen here with mountain climber Don Whillans, who made his home and many friends in Rawtenstall. (S. and L. Longworth)

Two of Jon's long standing dreams were to see the setts relaid on Daisy Hill and to save Ilex Mill from demolition. Both, thanks to English Heritage, have come to fruition, the setts relaid as part of the town centre Conversation Area (R.F.P) (left) and Ilex Mill, seen here in 1982, being converted to apartments by P.J. Liveseys. (K.F.*)

Right: A resident of Prospect Hill, next to Beech Street, is Colin Bishop, who has long kept pigeons, chickens and geese in the small allotment on the lane up to Cribden. Colin is also a tireless worker for charity, having raised many hundreds of pounds for "Stepping Stones", a local Development Therapy Unit for children. (Colin Bishop)

Left: Henry Holt lived in Waterfoot and took over his father's building business at the age of 16. He was a mine of information on local buildings, and spent much of his retirement in the 1980s collecting bricks, at first from Rossendale but later from all over the world. His hobby eventually filled several lock-up garages, each brick carefully catalogued by his wife, Mary, seen with him here at their house on Bacup Road. The problems of disposing of this hoard after Henry died became national news, but most of it is believed to hve been acquired by Lancashire County Museums Service. (Lancashire Magazine).

In September 1982 a self-help group, "Rossendale Business Enterprise", set up the "Small Businesses Club". Surrounded by items of Rossendale's industrial past in the Weavers' Cottage are Jeff Butler, Brian Chicken, Roger Pearson, Jennifer Drury, Jane Stott and Melvin Price. (R.C.T.)

The little garden outside the Weavers' Cottage holds several plants and bushes given in memory of members and friends. This one, held by Chairman Charles Ashmore, was planted by the Townswomen's Guild in the 1980s. (R.C.T.)

For a few years in the late 1980s and early 1990s, Rawtenstall Civic Society held a "Best Back Yard" competition to encourage imaginitive use of small spaces in the local back streets. It is difficult to get much smaller than the back stone balcony, beautifully presented by the ladies in sheltered accomodation at Old Row on Haslingden Road. (K.F.*)

Slowly, within the last fifteen years or so, Rawtenstall has begun to be proud of itself again, and a series of "Spring Clean" events were organised in the 1980s involving schools, families and neighbours. Civic Society Vice-Chairman Alan Edmondson and his grandsons David and Gareth contribute to the "Rubbish Mountain" collected as part of Civic Trust Environment week in 1989. (R.C.T.)

Rawtenstall Tutorial Centre, along with many other groups, made quite a party out of the weekend. (R.C.T.)

The new area Roman Catholic Secondary School on Haslingden Road was at first known as St. Ambrose, but later became All Saints. It provided space, with playing fields that could be used for church events. One of the most popular and regular visitors has been the race horse Desert Orchid, pictured here with Mayor Alan Fishwick, Mayoress Marie Fishwick and Father David Lupton. (David Lupton.)

St. James-the-Less R.C. Church was the setting for the marriage of England footballer Phill Neville and local girl Julie Killelea, bringing the full Manchester United team, including the Beckhams, to a rainy Rawtenstall in December 1999. Phil, second from left, and Julie, fourth from right, have become benefactors of local sporting facilities, and the plans for a £25,000 all-weather pitch in Whitaker Park are being inspected here with Ibby Khan, Rossendale's Sports Officer. (R.F.P.)

Brian Boys and his sons John, Michael and Peter have run the family firm for forty years, and as well building new properties, have pioneered restoration and re-use of our older buildings, including St. James' Waterfoot and the former Haslingden Road Methodist Church, now a Conference centre. Based in Waterfoot, they now carry out work over a wide area of the North West. (Brian Boys)

The battle between conservation and development is being fought out keenly in Rawtenstall. In March 2002, Oxana Metiuk, owner of the former Greenbank Estate Gate House, made a determined stand to prevent removal of the central gatepost for access to land allocated for building. Although the building has gone ahead, the future of the gatepost still (2003)lies in the balance. (R.F.P.)

A group of children take a break on a walk over the hills -the fresh air and healthy breezes have always been said to be a reason for the good singing voices of local people. It was certainly true in this case; the little girl at the top left is Rawtenstall's own Jane Horrocks. (Barbara Horrocks)

The Rossendale Male Voice Choir has now been joined by the Rossendale Ladies Choir, who them selves have proved formidable competitors on the Choir scene. Under their conductress, Beatrice Wade, they give regular performances both alone and with the Male Voice Choir. They have also been the guests of MGV Songerbung in three successful visits to Rossendale's twin town of Bocholt. (R.C.T.)

Above: In 1989 Rossendale appointed its first "Town Crier", Joe Grime, a local historian who made a significant contribution to the recently opened Pennine Bridleway. Joe is seen here with his son Kevin, as Robin Hood, at Waterfoot Medieval Fair on September 3rd 1989. (K.F.*)

Rossendale's present Town Crier and Toast-Master is Peter Gill, F.I.C.T.C., F.R.G.T.M., who not only presides over but helps organise many local events and represents Rossendale in gatherings across the country. The plaque on the stone outside Rawtenstall Station commemorates the 40th anniversary of "Town Twinning" with Bocholt. (Peter Gill)

For the 50th anniversary, a commemorative sculpture in the form of interlocking jigsaw puzzle pieces was unvieled on the space opposite the market. It has created a lot of interest and sisters Olivia and Madeline certainly found it a great attraction. (K.F.*)

The once overworked and polluted River Irwell is now the route of a major Sculpture Trail. This now locally famous "Tin Tree" was made by Bernard Tindall, and as a beech, the symbol of Bocholt, it stands on the corner of Bocholt Way. (K.F.*)

Another sculpture, "Gateway", stands by the path alongside the railway line, echoing the engineering of both the trains and the mills. (K.F.*)

Above and right: The 1960s by-pass made it possible to close Bank Street off for special occasions. In recent years, the most regular of these has been the annual Motor Bike Show, started by Tony Winder, when over 25, 000 visitors pack the town with bikes of all types, stalls, displays and events. Preparation for the event takes place over the whole year, and despite the vast number of people attending, there has never been any serious problem. It is an occasion for many voluntary groups to join in with marshalling and support, with all profits going to local Charities. (K.F.*)

In June 2002 the Queen's East Lancashire Regiment was given the Freedom of the Borough, and the right to march through the town. Once again, the whole street was given over to a spectacular display. (K.F.*)

Amongst the former local servicemen taking part was Walter Whittaker, former Chairman of Rossendale Sports Council, and instigator of the annual "Round the HIlls" walk. Sport in Rossendale certainly owes a great deal to his efforts, and spectators took this occasion to show their appreciation. (K.F.*)

Rossendale's Mayor, Jimmy Eaton, performs the ceremony at the junction of Bank Street and Kay Street, in front of the Unitarian Church and Barclay's Bank. (F.T.*)

The residents of Lumb created a Millenium Green for the year 2000, now a focal point for walkers and on the route of the Pennine Bridleway. This was the day the job took off, with Resident's Committee Chairman Brian Haslam receiving the cheque for £29,818 from the Countryside Commission's Liz Newton, February 17th 1998. Mayor Peter Heyworth and Ward Councillor Jean Haylor (behind him, right) joined with the children of the village Rainbow group for the presentation. (R.F.P.)

Water Village community held their 2003 Fete in the Schoolyard, this stall staffed by one of the oldest inhabitants, Mary Bird, who has lived in the village all her life. Wearing sunglasses is local Councillor Bill Riley (K.F.*)

The 2002 Golden Jubilee brought out the fun in many local schools. At St. Paul's Constable Lee fancy dress day, a young "Winston Churchill" presides over Rawtenstall's contribution to England's green and pleasant land , with Cribden Hill in the background. (K.F.*)

Rossendale's M.P. Janet Anderson joins the 2003 St. George's Day Parade from Whitaker Park to All Saints School along Haslingden Road. Janet regularly attends local events in a friendly capacity as well as the Valley's Parliamentary representative. (K.F.*)

Based in Waterfoot, the travelling theatre company "Horse and Bamboo" give Rossendale its live experience of modern street theatre. This event in 1998 was in celebration of the River Irwell, showing how its presence had shaped the history of the area, from rural stream to powering the great god Industry, and from pollution to once more sustaining fish and wild life along its course. The procession, seen here on New Hall Hey Road, wound its way to the Groundwork Countryside Centre by New Hall Hey Mill, where "Lady Irwell" regained her lost Kingdom. (Bob Frith).

Tailpiece. John B. Taylor captured this moment of peace in Rawtenstall's constantly changing scene before the mill lodges were drained at New Hall Hey. The 20th century has seen the town expand beyond the expectations of the early Corporation, and the industrial scene they knew has all but disappeared, but hopefully enough remains of the traditional spirit of the town to guide and inspire the makers of the 21st century.